Praise for *Beginning Mindfulness*

"A skillfully conceived book that guides and inspires new and experienced practitioners."

— Joan Halifax Roshi, Upaya Zen Center

"My relationship with Andrew JiYu Weiss has always been inspirational, his support and guidance always beneficial. My hope is that those who read this book will benefit as much as I have from meeting and knowing him."

— Claude AnShin Thomas, author of
Ending War, Living Peace: A Soldier's Journey

"Andrew Weiss is a gentle and compassionate guide to how to live with awareness in every moment. His book is a down-to-earth manual on how to apply mindfulness to practical, concrete situations of daily life. It grew out of handouts he created for an adult education class, and one could not ask for a better laboratory for testing out the efficacy of mindfulness practice. The concern in this and similar laboratory testing is not with Buddhist teachings per se but with how the stresses of daily life in a complex physical and social environment are addressed. Andrew has had his training in the two meditative traditions of Zen and Thich Nhat Hanh. The forcefulness of Zen in cutting through confused thinking is balanced by the gentle awareness practices of Thich Nhat Hanh in Andrew's presentation of mindfulness. It is a lovely, delightful book, one you would want to give to your friends and relatives who may have never heard of Buddhist mindfulness practice without any fear of offending their sensibilities."

— Mu Soeng, director of the Barre Center for Buddhist
Studies an~~d~~
Transforming t

"Andrew Weiss's book has been a tremendous resource for my students. Its lessons were easily read and put into practice by newcomers to mindfulness. Experienced practitioners found in them new approaches that expanded their range of practice and insights that deepened their experience of familiar practices. Its thoroughness and clarity make this text appropriate for study by teacher-less groups, and it can be profitably used by individuals as well."

— Richard Brady, Dharma teacher
and mathematics teacher, Sidwell Friends School

"Enlightened readers will be forever grateful that Andrew Weiss sat down to write *Beginning Mindfulness.* He is a master teacher, and he has given us a guide to the practice of meditation that is not only easy to follow but also a joy to read."

— Peter Rand, author of *China Hands*

"This is a beautiful book. It is a gift, an offering by a humble man imbued with the true spirit of teaching and helping. Andrew's deep understanding of mindfulness is steeped in his own experience over many years of practice, so every word rings true. There is great knowledge here, and also great love — love of his subject, his teachers, and the reader. *Beginning Mindfulness* is a dear, direct communication from the author's mind and heart to the reader's mind and heart — and it works: when you've finished this book, you understand mindfulness, it's in your life, you're on your way."

— Robert M. Alter, author of *How Long
Till My Soul Gets It Right?*

BEGINNING
MINDFULNESS

ANDREW WEISS

BEGINNING MINDFULNESS

LEARNING THE WAY OF AWARENESS

A TEN-WEEK COURSE

NEW WORLD LIBRARY
NOVATO, CALIFORNIA

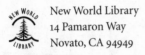

New World Library
14 Pamaron Way
Novato, CA 94949

Cover design by Cathey Flickinger
Interior design by Tona Pearce Myers

Library of Congress Cataloging-in-Publication Data
Weiss, Andrew.
  Beginning mindfulness : learning the way of awareness / by Andrew Weiss.
    p.   cm.
Includes bibliographical references and index.
  ISBN 1-57731-441-7 (pbk. : alk. paper)
  1. Meditation. I. Title.
  BL627.W419 2004
  204'.35—dc22   2003024035

First printing, March 2004
ISBN 1-57731-441-7
Printed in Canada on 100% postconsumer waste recycled paper
Distributed to the trade by Publishers Group West

10 9 8 7 6 5 4

*I offer this book
to my teachers,
and to my parents.*

Without them, I would not be.

CONTENTS

ACKNOWLEDGMENTS

In 1995, I had the honor to inherit an adult education mindfulness meditation class from Larry Rosenberg and Harrison "Hob" Hoblitzelle, two of the most outstanding teachers of Insight Meditation in the United States. Theirs are very big footsteps, and I am grateful to them both for their faith, encouragement, and guidance.

This book is a memorial to Hob Hoblitzelle, my mentor and friend who died in 2001. We lost a great teacher and inspiring guide, and I miss him. Without his faith in me and his guidance and generosity, this book would not exist.

My thanks also to the Cambridge Center for Adult Education, which has kept offering this course whether I had six or sixteen people enrolled, and to the many people who have taken the class and taught me about how the practice of mindfulness works in daily life.

I could not have written this book, or be who I am, without my teachers:

Thanks to the late Zen Master Su Bong (Mu Deung Sunim), who compassionately doused me with the cold water of the teachings and saw things in me that I didn't see in myself. I recall especially his dedication, single-mindedness, love, and impish sense of humor. His presence has continued with me since his death.

Thanks to Su Bong's and my teacher, Zen Master Seung Sahn, who for years had the uncanny habit of showing up in my life just when I needed him. Seung Sahn is a true Zen master, and everyone who has studied with him, whether it be me or Jon Kabat-Zinn or Larry Rosenberg, all show the mark of his teachings. The "Fourth Week" section of this book would be impossible without him.

Thanks to the Venerable Thich Nhat Hanh, whose teaching and practice styles have been so meaningful in my life and who for many years was my beacon in the darkness.

Thanks to Baghwan Nityananda, the great Siddha, who first showed me what grace is.

Thanks to Claude AnShin Thomas, who has unwavering faith in me and the willingness to confront my most pernicious habits. I am grateful for his sustaining friendship and his patient teaching.

Thanks to Sharon Turner and Sarah Smith, the teachers of the Awakenings clairvoyant program, who have taught me the importance of staying in my body and the skills to do it, who have helped erase years of authoritarian imprint on my life, and who have helped me change my life in ways I never thought possible.

Thanks to my many friends in the mindfulness meditation community in Greater Boston, especially Elizabeth Wood, Sue Bridge, Bich and Chi Nguyen, Olivia Hoblitzelle, and Miriam Hawley and Jeffrey McIntyre; to my fellow practitioners in the Clock Tower Sangha in Maynard, Massachusetts, especially Nancy Buchinsky, Tina Weiner, Peter Cutler, Vicki Haskell, Joan Kimball, Susan Phillips, Sally Bubier, and Cal Andrews; and to my dharma friend Daeja Napier. All of them have sustained me with their practice and nurtured my growth.

Thanks also to Arnold Kotler, the founder and former publisher and editor at Parallax Press, and his wife, Therese Fitzgerald, for their support, generosity, and encouragement. They are both fine teachers and offer their support to us through DharmaFriends in Hawaii.

Many thanks to Richard Brady of the Washington (D.C.) Mindfulness Community for his faith in this book and his invaluable assistance and support in getting it out to the world.

Thanks to George Bowman, who, whatever his faults, was my steady, loving guide in practice every week for many years.

Thanks to my good friend Peter Rand for his friendship and caring and for encouraging me to see the value of this book and to pursue publication. Peter generously edited this manuscript, and his many suggestions were essential in making this a readable, coherent book.

And especially, the deepest bow of gratitude to my wonderful wife, Avril Rama, for her humor, understanding, and deep dedication to a spiritual life, and for inviting me to add her world of meditation practice in Siddha Yoga to my deep Buddhist roots.

A deep bow of appreciation to the team at New World Library: my editor Jason Gardner, who has gracefully shepherded this book to publication and has been a joy to work with; Barbara King, whose copy edits made the book cleaner and more consistent; Cathey Flickinger, who designed the gorgeous cover; and Tona Pearce Myers, who has made the book a beautiful visual reflection of its contents.

INTRODUCTION

Many wonderful books describe the path of mindfulness meditation, but few offer basic, simple instruction to dedicated beginners on the path. This book is designed to offer that kind of instruction.

This book began as a series of handouts for an eight-week (now ten-week) class called "Living the Way of Awareness: Mindfulness Meditation for Everyday Life." Like the course from which it grew, this book is divided into ten short sections. Over ten weeks, you will develop a steady sitting and walking meditation practice, one that integrates meditation and mindfulness with your life. Each section includes some basic instruction in mindfulness meditation practice and some "home play" assignments. If you want the full benefit of this book, I suggest you approach it sequentially.

Mindfulness meditation was developed by Gautama Siddhartha, whom we call the Buddha, about 2,600 years ago. The Buddha (the word *buddha* means "one who is awake") offered mindfulness as a practical way to develop our ability to see clearly, to understand ourselves and others better, so that we might live a more joyful and fulfilling life. The Buddha saw how our ideas about things get in our way and realized that the best idea about life is no idea at all. The teachings of the Buddha, in their earliest and original form, are remarkably free of doctrine. While they embrace the same fundamental truths that are present in all the world's great religions, they offer no religious creed for people to believe in. Instead, the Buddha provided a way to use our personal experience to guide us to awakening.

The Buddha is not a god or a being to be worshiped. You do not have to become a Buddhist to practice mindfulness in a nonsectarian context. You can be a Christian, a Jew, a Hindu, or an agnostic and still practice the Buddha's teachings on mindfulness without any conflict. I refer to the Buddha's teachings throughout this book; in fact, this book would not be possible without them. But I have absorbed those teachings in my experience living as a North American in the late twentieth century from a middle-class family with deep roots in Judaism. My family's ancestors were Jewish residents of the *shtetls* of Eastern Europe. Some residents were deeply spiritual, others were not; probably they were all poor. My background is very different from the Buddha's, who was an Indian prince of a royal family and next in succession to his father's throne. Even so, the Buddha's teachings speak directly to me. I find that I can practice them without having to abandon my ancestral spiritual roots, without giving up one iota of who I am. If anything, as I practice mindfulness, my sense of who I am and my connection to my spiritual roots become clearer and clearer.

Meditation is not just something you do on a cushion or chair. Anything you do is an occasion to engage yourself mindfully in the present moment. When you engage mindfulness meditation in the present moment, it makes everything you do in your daily life sacred and full of meaning, even washing the dishes or turning on an electric light.

Ultimately, the path of mindfulness will lead you to a place within yourself where you may encounter the world without ideas or preconceptions, where you can disengage from your habitual narrative and free yourself from mental constructs. Here you will see yourself and the world as we all really are, in our great, infinite radiance and tenderness, and in our most awful delusions. Mindfulness allows us to experience the delight of touching life deeply and authentically. It gives us a way through suffering to joy. It encourages us to do all of this every moment in our daily lives.

Faith will be important as you pursue the path of mindfulness. Often you will notice that your practice of mindfulness yields immediate fruits. You will also encounter periods of confusion, when your meditation seems all wrong, or when it seems you are getting nothing out of it. Faith is what sustains us when those inevitable, but challenging, periods crop up. I have encountered a description of faith by Richard and Antra Borofsky that I find useful:

> Faith is not a belief, nor is it based on reason. Faith is a choice we make to enter into things as they are and to work with and learn from whatever is happening, no matter how impossible it may seem. It

is a choice we make to open ourselves to possibilities that are unseen and unknown.

Your faith in your capacity to be honestly and sincerely open to this moment will guide you along the path of mindfulness to help you wake up. Your faith in the practices of mindfulness, in the unerring rightness of what this moment offers you, will help you walk through many doors that otherwise might be closed to you.

People use mindfulness for many purposes, and you may employ it to reduce stress or to manage pain. These are legitimate and important ways to use mindfulness. They are not, however, the focus of what you will learn and practice in this book. Mindfulness meditation, in its pure and classic sense, is about finding your true self. It is about waking up to the true nature of the present moment. As you look deeply into yourself and other beings in the world, you will have the opportunity to free yourself from the concepts that you have about everything, including who you are. As you begin to live this way, being authentically who you are and in direct contact with the world, you will transform the areas of your suffering and make your life more vibrant. Stress reduction and pain management will happen along the way; they are helpful by-products.

Many traditions have developed around the Buddha's teachings. My introduction to meditation began in the so-called Therevadan or insight tradition. I then gravitated toward the Zen practices that have come to the United States from Korea and Japan. When the Zen monk Thich Nhat Hanh introduced me to his Vietnamese blending of these two traditions, he brought together for me the best of both worlds.

I offer here the practices of mindfulness that I have adapted for my own use. They draw on the Therevadan teachings, particularly in the use of guided meditations and in the techniques for establishing mindfulness in our breathing, our bodies, our feelings, and our thinking. They draw even more strongly on the Zen exhortation to realize our true, clear, and spacious original nature right now in the present moment, to enter deeply and directly into the heart of our present experience, and to dissolve the barrier between the observer and what is being observed. For me, the keynote of good mindfulness practice is a lack of self-consciousness. The best mindfulness practice is one that is most engaged, spontaneous, natural, and free.

If, after all this introduction, you have an idea of what mindfulness meditation practice is, I encourage you to throw it out the window as the first step on your true path of mindfulness. The Buddha used to say that the teachings of mindfulness are a raft that takes us over the waters from the shore of delusion to the shore of awakening. It would be silly, he reminds us, to worship the raft or to carry it around on dry land.

REMEMBER: *Go Slowly, Breathe, and Smile!*

How to Use This Book

Weekly Sections

Each of the ten sections in this book includes practice instruction and suggested exercises. The best way to use the book is to read the practice instructions and to then do the exercises in that section for at least one week before going on to the next one. The introduction gives an overview of the book and of mindfulness practice, and I suggest you read it before starting the first section.

Even if you think you've mastered the exercises in one section and are impatient to go ahead to the next, or want to skip ahead to a section that especially appeals to you, please do your best to become aware of your impatience or boredom and stick with that week's home play. Your boredom and impatience can be a doorway to deepening practice and greater understanding. Just do your best to notice these feelings with as little self-judgment as you can — or if you have self-critical thoughts, try to be aware of them, too. Everything is grist for the mindfulness mill, so don't throw anything out.

In my class we do all of these exercises in ten weeks,

but you can be more flexible than that. If you want to spend two weeks doing the guided meditation on mindfulness of the body, for example, please do so. Your guidepost for going on can be "Do I feel comfortably established and grounded in this section's practice?" If you do, go on to the next section. Take your time, and be easy on yourself.

You will find it useful to finish all of the sections in this book before going on to other kinds of practice. I have designed the readings and exercises in *Beginning Mindfulness* to give you a basic grounding in most of the skills you will need to practice mindfulness successfully. Please don't omit steps or stop partway.

OTHER BOOKS

This book is very basic and simple. You can augment the readings in this book by adding another book or two if you wish. If you do this, stick with the structure of this book's exercises and use the other books as encouragements in the practice.

I would recommend only a few books for this purpose: Thich Nhat Hanh's *Miracle of Mindfulness;* Jon Kabat-Zinn's *Wherever You Go, There You Are;* and Jerry Braza's *Moment by Moment.* All three are listed in "Recommended Reading" at the end of this book.

A GROUP PRACTICING TOGETHER

If you can organize a group to practice the "course" this book offers, you will gain valuable support in establishing and deepening your mindfulness practice. The best way to learn mindfulness meditation and practice is with a group. In groups, we can assist one another and benefit from each other's wisdom and experience. The synergy of the group process also accelerates learning and deepens our meditation practice. We can get and give encouragement in a group. We also discover that many of the issues that each of us faces in mindfulness practice are often the same, even when they may not seem to be.

The old allegory of the three blind men who encounter an elephant for the first time beautifully demonstrates the way a group works together in the practice of mindfulness. One of the blind men, grasping the elephant's leg, thinks an elephant is sturdy and strong, like a tree. Another, holding its trunk, decides that it is strong, flexible, and supple like a snake. The third, fingering its tail, is sure the elephant is feathery and delicate like a feather duster. All of us in a group have a piece of the truth, like the three blind men. It is a great joy and benefit to share our piece with others and to have others open the window of awakening a little further for us.

What Works

Several sections in this book use guided meditations as their primary instruction tool. I have organized these guided meditations to help you develop the skills you will need to handle the thoughts and feelings that naturally arise in sitting meditation and in daily-life mindfulness.

Some people really like guided meditations; others find them difficult. If you like guided meditations, then use them just as they are. If you find that the guided meditations get on your nerves, you can extract from them the direction in which you need to focus during your sitting practice. But I must admit that the second approach is a bit more dangerous than the first because the guided meditation helps to keep us on track.

Like most meditation teachers, I am presenting the practices that work for me. They may not all work for you. You and I are not the same person, and the point of practicing mindfulness is not for you to become like me: It is for you to become more and more fully your own self. So go with what works for you. You can adapt the exercises in each section of this book to a guided or nonguided format. What is most important is to go through the stages of learning about the breath, about the body, about thoughts, feelings, and the objects of our concentration, and then to enter into the heart-expanding practices of loving-kindness and compassion. My home play exercises at the end of each section are suggestions. Please adapt them so they work well for you.

Many of us are afraid that if we really allow ourselves to be in the present moment, we will meet some terrible part of ourselves or encounter a great deal of pain and suffering. That may happen; suffering is part of life. But we may meet joy there as well. Joy and suffering are companions; if we want to know one, we will inevitably get to know the other. Hob Hoblitzelle liked to remind people that joy can arrive any time, unannounced, and dance on our eyelashes. As you do these practices, please allow yourself the opportunity to experience both joy and suffering. They are essential elements of mindfulness practice, just as they are of daily life.

PART ONE

BEGINNING
MINDFULNESS

GETTING STARTED

The first step in starting a mindfulness practice is to establish the basic elements. These include mindfulness of breathing, sitting meditation, and daily-life mindfulness. In this chapter, you will learn how to use your breathing to establish mindfulness and increase your awareness. You will also learn the basics of sitting meditation and get suggestions for creating your own daily-life mindfulness practice. In each subsequent chapter in this section, you will build on the practices you learn here and add new ones, so by the fourth week you will have the essentials of mindfulness practice in place.

Mindfulness practice comes in two varieties: formal and informal. The formal practice is what we would normally call "meditation," for which we set aside a specific time to sit silently with mindful awareness of our breathing, or to walk slowly and silently with mindful awareness of our breath and our walking. The informal practice involves mindfulness of our daily-life activities, and is just as much "meditation" as the formal practices are. Because the heart of mindfulness practice is the enactment of

mindfulness in everything in our lives, both the formal
and informal practices of mindfulness are equally important. Each supports the other. Without formal practice, it
is difficult to develop a deep understanding of our minds
and our true nature as living beings. Formal practice gives
us a controlled, simplified environment where we can
encounter ourselves and the world in the present
moment. Informal practice puts mindfulness into every
act and increases our concentration and awareness.
Without informal practice, we would develop split per-
sonalities, with one deeper level of awareness when we are
doing sitting or walking meditation and another less open
level of awareness at other times.

DAILY FORMAL PRACTICE

Doing some formal mindfulness practice every day is
important. It strengthens our concentration and gives us
the opportunity to do nothing and to be present in the
moment. *Be* is the operative word here: *be* and not *do*. We
all have plenty of "do-ing" in our lives, and not enough
"be-ing." We need both. Not only do we encounter ourselves and the world differently when we are be-ing rather
than do-ing, we also learn quickly that the secret to living
well is to "be" in the center of our "do-ing." Or to put it
another way, we learn that the secret to an awakened life is
to be completely, deeply still, expansive and present in the
heart of whatever we are doing. We stop, come to rest.
Only when we can rest from our mind's constant running
can we be present to this moment.

The first formal meditation practice you will learn is sitting meditation.

SITTING MEDITATION

Meditation teacher Arnie Kotler likes to say that sitting meditation accomplishes two things: It allows us to get to know ourselves, and it improves our concentration. Getting to know ourselves means looking deeply into our own nature and the nature of everything around us, and cultivating our willingness to allow our preconceptions about ourselves and our lives, and about everything else, to fall away. As we get to know better the true nature of our minds, we start to understand that thoughts are thoughts and feelings are feelings, and to become less invested in the drama that our thoughts and feelings can so easily create. We begin to live more gracefully.

Mindfulness meditation is not about being in a trance, or about escaping from reality. It is about waking up. We spend most of our lives caught up in the conceptual knowledge we have acquired, and in our concepts of who we are, or what our lives mean, or what a tree is or what a boulder is, and so on and on. This layer of concept sits between us and the reality of the present moment. To touch the present moment, we must allow this layer of concept to drop away. To allow this layer to drop away, we first have to be able to stop. We have to stop both body and mind. Only when our minds stop racing, only when we allow ourselves to be in one place, can we truly be present in the here and now. This is the first step we take in mindfulness meditation: We use mindfulness of breathing as a way to help us stop and truly be here. As we continue to practice mindfulness meditation, our capacity to stop and be present increases. Out of this we naturally develop deeper concentration and the capacity to look deeply into ourselves or into whatever we encounter.

This process of looking deeply is not analytical. It is spontaneous and unstudied. We don't have to figure anything out or make anything happen. All we need do is to sit, be aware of our breathing, and allow our concentration and mindfulness to penetrate whatever comes along.

In sitting meditation we begin by focusing our attention on our breathing. If we can truly be present with our in-breath and out-breath, we have stopped ourselves in the present moment, allowed our concept about what breathing is to fall away, and begun to touch the true nature of breathing. If we stay concentrated on our breathing, we will notice that our breathing changes, that no two breaths are exactly the same, and that other things, like thoughts and feelings, arise and ask for our attention. In this way we come to know ourselves, our feelings, and our minds directly, in a way that sits outside conceptual knowledge.

Posture

To do sitting meditation well, you need a good and stable posture. If you sit in a chair, sit with your back straight so that your legs are at a 90-degree angle (or as close to one as you can put them) and with your feet flat on the floor. If you are sitting on a cushion, sit with your legs crossed or in a half-lotus position (or if you are really flexible, in a full-lotus) and with your back straight. It is helpful to have the cushion tilt your buttocks forward slightly to stabilize the base of your spine. Please do not lean against the back of a chair or against a wall, because if you do, you are likely to go to sleep.

Your arms should be near, but not touching, your sides. Make sure you are not pressing against your chest; this will inhibit your breathing. Your chin should be slightly tucked in. Your hands can be in any comfortable posture.

You can close your eyes during sitting meditation, or if you wish, you can keep them slightly open, with your gaze adjusted to about a 45-degree angle and directed at the floor in front of you. If you keep your eyes open, here are two important pointers: do not let your eyes wander, and gaze softly — don't drill a hole in the floor with your eyes.

Stillness in sitting is important. When we allow our bodies to stop, our bodies are still. Stillness of body contributes to stillness of mind. If you move your arms, legs, head, or hands, you will disturb the stopping of your mind and the stability of your sitting meditation. You may also disturb the other people with whom you may be sitting. If you must move because you have a muscle cramp or a pain somewhere, and the pain is interfering with your stability, please take this as an opportunity to practice mindfulness of movement by moving slowly and with awareness of each movement of your bones and muscles.

Breathing

In mindfulness meditation we naturally develop abdominal or belly breathing. You can experience this by holding your hand on your abdomen and feeling it rise and fall with each breath. Focusing our breathing in our abdomens puts our attention and our breath deep in our bodies and creates stability. So as a beginner you may want to hold your hand over your belly and feel your breath to connect you with your breathing.

Beyond doing some simple breathing exercises that are explained below, we don't try to control our breath in sitting meditation. It's important to notice the breath free of our conscious control. Simple awareness of breathing is all you need. You are already breathing, so just notice it. If you notice how your breath is right now, whether it is long or short, deep or shallow, you are becoming aware of your breathing.

You will notice in meditation that the place of your breath and the nature of your breathing will change depending on the stability of your concentration and the nature of the thoughts or feelings that arise. You will notice this particularly with stressful thoughts and feelings, particularly fear and anxiety. Your breath will tend to rise up into the area around your heart or perhaps even higher in your chest. If you find yourself anxious or upset, abdominal breathing will stabilize your feelings. You can use abdominal breathing this way even if you aren't doing sitting meditation.

When you find yourself getting sleepy, focus your breathing at the tip of your nose. This will move your attention, and your blood, up to your head, and after a few minutes the sleepiness should go away. Then you can allow your breathing to move wherever it will.

If you find that you are being distracted, you might try taking very deep in-breaths, holding the breath slightly after the inhalation, and then exhaling slowly. Breathing like this for a few minutes will restore your concentration to your breathing, and you can then let your breath come and go as it will. This exercise also works well if you find yourself controlling your breathing.

Please remember that all you are doing here is noticing that you are breathing. You aren't trying to breathe — you are already doing that. You are simply allowing yourself to be aware of your breath.

Don't set unrealistic goals for yourself. If you do sitting practice for five minutes after you wake up in the morning and five minutes before you go to bed, it will help you. Once you see the benefits of sitting practice, you may find it easier and more natural to spend a little more time at it.

Your Practice Environment

To support your formal sitting practice at home, try to find a special place. You don't need much room, just a place for a cushion or chair, and perhaps some beautiful object you enjoy looking at, such as a small vase of flowers or a plant or a rock or a carving. Try to use this space only for your meditation practice: It will help you to meditate every time you sit down there. Remember, sitting meditation should be enjoyable and rewarding. If it isn't, you won't want to do it, so make the space as inviting as possible. If your back permits, try to make sure that your meditation setup encourages you to keep your back straight without the support of a wall or chair back.

You will benefit from establishing a special time of day for formal meditation practice, just as you benefit from creating a special place for it. Try to do your sitting meditation at the same time every day. If you're a morning person, try sitting before breakfast. If you're an evening person, sit about two hours after dinner. If you do formal walking meditation (a practice you will encounter in the next section), either inside or outside, try to do it at the same time every day. This kind of discipline really helps.

Counting the Breath

One of the most basic exercises we do in mindfulness meditation we call "counting" our breathing. The purpose of this exercise is to help us to be truly aware that when we are breathing in, we are breathing in, and that when we are breathing out, we are breathing out. Does this sound simpleminded? Consider for a moment how often during the day you are actually aware of your breathing. The answer probably is, not much. One good way for us to start developing awareness of breathing is to count our breaths from one to ten, and then from ten back to one. I suggest that you do this by saying to yourself silently the word *in* during your in-breath, and then the word *one* when your breath turns from the in-breath to the out-breath. Next, say to yourself the word *out* during your out-breath, and then *one* when your breath turns from the out-breath to the in-breath. On the next in-breath, say, "In, two," and then "Out, two," and so on up to ten. Then do it in reverse. Start with "In, ten" and "Out, ten," and go back down to one. If you can keep your attention completely focused on your breathing for these twenty breaths, you have established good concentration. When you lose track of the numbers or of your breath, you should go back and start at "In, one" again.

If you judge yourself for not doing this exercise correctly, you are finding out some useful information about yourself. This is mindfulness in action: Your perfectionism is showing itself! To help you cut through the judgments, try considering the exercise as a game. It's like hopscotch: If you step outside the lines, go back to the beginning.

This simple counting exercise is an excellent way to begin any session of sitting meditation, no matter how experienced a meditator you may be. Once you have established your concentration by counting your breath, you can drop the numbers, and just say "in" on the in-breath and "out" on the out-breath. Now you can start to notice the quality of your in-breath and out-breath: long or short, deep or shallow, in the chest or in the abdomen, ragged or steady. You are already on the path of awareness.

INFORMAL PRACTICE:
DAILY-LIFE MINDFULNESS

The heart of mindfulness practice lies in imbuing each act and each moment with mindful attention. It is essential, therefore, for us to pay as exquisite attention as possible to our every thought and activity from moment to moment. This is daily-life mindfulness. It helps us to stop, and ultimately it becomes a different and profound way of life. If you focus entirely on a simple act, such as turning on the ignition of your car or putting the key in the lock of your front door, you will allow your mind to rest in the present moment and eventually attain a new and more complete understanding of yourself and the world. You get the point: This informal practice is critical.

Everything that you read in this book about formal practice applies equally to the informal practice of daily-life mindfulness. The act of washing dishes can be just as precious an opportunity to wake up as the time we spend doing sitting meditation. Being engaged in the moment means being present, no matter what we are doing. It means putting aside the tricks we use to hide from being right here right now and giving ourselves completely to whatever we are doing, whether it's walking or peeling a potato. One meditation teacher has described the process of mindfulness practice as the slow settling of water in a pond. As the pond settles, the water becomes clearer and clearer. In the same way, as we become more mindful, and our mind comes to rest more steadily, our understanding and true presence become clearer and clearer. For me, it is as though a veil has dropped away and I come into direct contact with myself and the world around me.

The concentration necessary for completely engaging in your daily activities is something you will cultivate over time, so please don't be discouraged if at first you find your attention wandering. As in formal meditation practice, you cannot expect your mind to stop completely when you engage yourself mindfully in daily life. The thoughts or feelings that may come up while you are mindfully engaged are important windows on understanding. They will provide their own opportunity for you to wake up. You will want to acknowledge them and be with them in an accepting, nonanalytical way, just as you do during sitting meditation.

Many of us find it helpful to use *gathas* — little poems — to encourage mindfulness of what we're doing. Some of these are included in part two of this book, and are for some common everyday acts, such as waking up in the morning, washing dishes, turning on the television, and so on. Please feel free to use others from the two books of gathas in the recommended reading list, or make up your own.

Here are some possible ways to reinforce mindfulness in your daily life. During your first week of practice, please pick one or two and give them your wholehearted attention. You can use conscious breathing — awareness of breath — as a foundation to encourage daily-life mindfulness, just as you use it as the foundation for your sitting and walking meditation practice. Each week's home play includes adding another daily-life mindfulness activity to your daily routine, so you will be referring back to this list frequently as you go along.

- When you wake up in the morning, allow yourself some slow, mindful breaths before you get out of bed. See if you can be aware of your breathing and of making the transition from sleeping to waking. Be aware of the sound, the quality of light, or the darkness. Feel each in-breath calm your body and mind, and each out-breath release any tension or thoughts you're holding. Try smiling and see what happens.

- As you rise from bed, be aware of your feet making contact with the floor. Notice how different your body feels in the lying-down, sitting, and standing postures. Be aware of your weight on your feet, of the floor supporting your body, and of the motion of your feet and legs as you begin to walk.

• Try eating breakfast without reading the newspaper or watching television. If possible, eat silently for all or part of your meal. Before you eat, allow yourself to breathe in and out three times and bring your awareness to the food in front of you.

• Take a few minutes, either at home or on your way to work, to notice something enjoyable about the morning: perhaps the sunlight or the rain or the face of a child or a flower or the sounds of birds or the wind. See if you can allow yourself and your surroundings to inhabit the same space.

• On your way to work or school, or to appointments or your other daily errands, try to be mindful of your traveling. Be aware of your walking, your sitting on the subway, your strap hanging on the bus, or your sitting while you are riding in a car. If you are driving a car or riding a bicycle or motorcycle, try to be aware of your driving or riding. Take a few mindful breaths to relax your body and mind. Do your best to allow your steps and actions to be peaceful ones.

• If you drive a car or ride a motorcycle or bicycle, use a few mindful breaths to calm you and bring you in tune with your vehicle and the act of driving or riding before you turn on the ignition or right after you mount your bike. Notice how you're holding your body, and let your breathing help you relax your shoulders, soften your face. See if you can break the pressure of pushing to get where you are going and simply enjoy the process of getting there. When you see a red traffic light, allow that to be a bell of mindfulness and an opportunity to come back to your breath; relax your face and see whether a smile is possible. When someone cuts you off, try using awareness of your breath to calm your anger and fear.

- When you get to work or school, or wherever you go on your daily tasks, practice some mindful breathing when you arrive and before you begin your work. If you are at a desk, try sitting down and taking some mindful breaths before taking out your work or talking with your fellow workers or students. If you are at a computer workstation, try taking three mindful breaths before turning on your computer. If you are shopping, pause before the entrance to the store and take three mindful breaths to calm and orient you before you walk in. Allow your body to relax before you begin, and see whether a smile is possible.

- Several times during the day, allow yourself to become aware of your breathing and re-center yourself. Use these occasions to become aware of your body and to let your breath quiet your mind. See if you can allow a smile to bloom.

- When you walk somewhere, try to be aware of your breathing and your steps. Are they peaceful steps or harsh ones? Can you allow yourself to slow down and make a trip to the bathroom an occasion for walking meditation?

- Many things happen every day that you can use as bells of mindfulness: the doorbell, the telephone, sounds on your computer, turning on a light, flushing a toilet, and so on. Let each one be an occasion to notice your breathing and allow some mindful in- and out-breaths. When the telephone rings, let it ring two or three times before you answer it. This is a great contradiction to our conditioning. Remember, if they really want to talk with you, they won't hang up! One of my students who spends a lot of time in meetings uses picking up his pencil as a bell of mindfulness and even had special pencils made up that have *Breathe* embossed on them.

- If you work on a computer, create a screen saver that encourages mindfulness — perhaps a photo of flowers or animals, or scrolling, suggestive words like *breathe* or *mindful every moment.* Play around with this. The Washington (D.C.) Mindfulness Community has a "mindful clock" program available on its website that can sound a bell on your computer hourly or every fifteen minutes as a reminder. This program is very effective and many of my computer-worker students love it. You can find it at www.mindfulnessdc.org.

- Approach your lunch and dinner with the same mindfulness with which you approached breakfast. A few mindful breaths before you start eating might be helpful. During the meal try to be aware of chewing your food. Pause between swallowing one bite of food and picking up the next one. Spend at least five minutes of your meal in silence. If you do have a conversation, keep the topics light and supportive; especially try to avoid arguments or angry exchanges.

- During your lunchtime, allow yourself some enjoyable time in addition to your meal. Talk with a friend, perhaps, or take a walk. Whatever you do, as you do it, see if you can be aware of your breathing. Slow yourself down, and relax.

- When you are ready to leave your day's activities, take a moment to appreciate what you've done that day in being mindful in your work or school or day's tasks. Consider how you can build on that the next day.

- Help to make your trip home a transition time by slowing down. Walk mindfully and be aware of your breathing. Try to allow a smile to be there. Notice the quality of the air, and see if you can accept it for what it is — cold, hot, wet, dry — without resisting it or trying to make it different. Allow your attention to be with your surroundings.

- Try being aware of your feelings and thoughts as you approach home, and take a few mindful breaths before you open the door. Make this transition a conscious one, and notice what it feels like to be home and how that feels different from being at work or school or at your daily tasks.

- If you watch television at night, why not turn down the sound during commercials or between programs? Close your eyes, and allow yourself some mindful breaths. Get up and take a mindful walk to the kitchen or bathroom. If you're reading, try stopping every half-hour. Close your eyes for a minute or so, and bring your attention back to your breath; become more aware of the room and the noises or silence of your home. If you're with your family, try giving yourself some mini-occasions to breathe mindfully and relax.

• If you have a bell of mindfulness in your house, you can encourage it to sound several times during the evening to slow yourself and your family down.

• As you go to bed and prepare for sleep, take some mindful breaths, become aware of the bed supporting you, and allow yourself a smile. Feel the muscles of your body relaxing as you sink into your bed. Try letting go of the past day's activities and of your anticipation of tomorrow. See whether you can end the day with a smile.

BELL OF MINDFULNESS

In my meditation classes we use a bell as one way to help us focus our attention. You can use this same tool at home. The bell can provide an enjoyable and easy way to share the practices of mindfulness with your family and to get their support. To do this, instruct your family members that each sound of the bell is a signal for them to stop what they are doing and to enjoy taking three in- and out-breaths. You can invite different family members to be responsible for sounding the bell at different times during the day or on different days. Every time the bell sounds, each member of your family will be reminded to return to his or her breathing, and this reminder will reinforce your mindfulness as well as the atmosphere of mindfulness in your household.

The kind of bell that we use in my meditation class is called a Japanese *rin* gong. It is a small bowl made of spun brass and comes with a small cushion and a small stick. We use the stick to "invite" the bell to sound. The stick is the "inviter."

The phrase *invite the bell to sound* comes from the Vietnamese language and custom. It suggests treating the bell with a lot more respect than the expressions *hitting the bell* or *striking the bell*. Would you hit or strike something or someone that you care about? Inviting the bell to sound creates a different, more mindful relationship.

When you invite the bell, here is a gatha you can use to help focus your attention. Say it silently to yourself, and coordinate each line with your breath:

Voice of the bell, voice of my heart,	(BREATHING IN)
I invite your sound to awaken me.	(BREATHING OUT)
May all beings live in mindfulness,	(BREATHING IN)
Our hearts open and minds clear.	(BREATHING OUT)

When you hear the bell, try saying this gatha silently to yourself:

Listen, listen . . .	(BREATHING IN)
The sound of this bell brings	
me back to my true self.	(BREATHING OUT)

Repeat this two-line gatha for three in- and out-breaths.

Keep the bell in a special place where everyone can find it. If you have children, it is especially helpful to let them be the keepers of the bell. Parents have told me that their children will invite the bell whenever there is tension in the house or whenever someone begins shouting or behaving in a hurtful way; the bell becomes the children's way of saying "Stop," and it is very helpful.

When you invite the bell, first touch the bell with the inviter and hold it on the bell, so you create a "stopped" sound. That's a signal that the bell is about to sound. Then, use the inviter to invite the bell to a full sound, and you and everyone around you can enjoy your breathing.

Anything that reminds us to bring our attention to the present moment is a true bell of mindfulness. Becoming aware of my discursive thinking or the sound of the telephone ringing, engaging in daily-life mindfulness activities of any type — all have the capacity to assist me to be in the present moment, to be truly mindful. The next time you find that your mind is wandering, try returning to your breath; you return to the present moment, and mindfulness is there, even if only for an instant. Doing this is a key to good practice.

Home Play

FORMAL PRACTICE: Create a sitting meditation place for yourself at home. Try doing sitting meditation for five minutes in the morning after you get up and for five minutes in the evening, either after dinner or before bed-time. See whether you are a morning sitter or an evening sitter. Perhaps you are both! Morning sitting sets us up well for our day. Evening sitting helps us clear the thoughts and feelings that have come up during the day. During your five minutes of sitting, try using the exercise of counting the breath.

INFORMAL PRACTICE: Take one item from the list of daily-life mindfulness activities. Do your best to remain mindful every time you do that activity throughout the week. Notice how your relationship to that activity changes over time with your mindful attention.

GOING DEEPER

SITTING AND BREATHING

During his lifetime the Buddha wrote two essential "how-to" texts about mindfulness meditation practice. The first, and the most fundamental, is "The Sutra on the Full Awareness of Breathing." *Sutra* is the Sanskrit word for a sacred text that contains important teachings.

In this sutra the Buddha shows us how we can use awareness of our breath — breathing in and breathing out — to take us all the way from the rocky shoals of confusion to the smooth sands of serenity. He proposes a series of exercises to accomplish this. The first step, he tells us, is to be aware of the nature and quality of our breath.

We can begin by being aware of whether our in-breath is long or short. Perhaps our in-breath is short and our out-breath is long. It's not important to make our breath be a particular way; it's only important to notice how our breath is.

We train our attention on this breath that we are breathing right now and not on remembering the one we have just breathed. We also do not anticipate the one we will inhale or exhale next. To maintain this attention, some of us find it helpful to concentrate on the point where our breathing turns from in-breath to out-breath. In this momentary pause, the in-breath is finished, the out-breath hasn't yet begun, and our attention can come to rest.

Then we can become aware of whether our breathing is deep or shallow. Does the depth of our breathing change as we do our sitting or walking meditation for longer periods of time?

Then we can inquire, How do we feel when our breathing is shallow? When it is deep? What thoughts or feelings arise as we are focused on our breathing? Can we see that a certain quality of breathing associates itself with a certain thought or feeling? Here is one example: If we are frightened, our breathing will naturally be shallow and rapid, and will locate itself in our upper chest. In most of our lives, usually we are aware, first, that we are scared; then, perhaps, we notice how we are breathing, or even whether we are breathing! When we are practicing mindfulness of breathing, the process is reversed: We first become aware that our breathing is shallow and rapid. Once we notice the quality of our breathing, then we can inquire, What goes along with our shallow and rapid breathing? Once we've asked the question, the answer is clear and obvious: We're frightened.

For right now, you only have to be aware of the quality of your breathing and the thought or feeling that may come up. Remember, the focus is on the breath, not on the thought or feeling. For this week, when you find your attention has wandered from your breathing, you can just recognize that you are thinking and return to your breathing again.

Our approach here resembles Björn Borg's approach to tennis: to get the ball over the net one more time than his opponent. Likewise, we do our best to return to our breathing one more time than our minds wander. But our approach to coming back to our breath should be anything other than that of a battle or contest. You can help yourself by being aware of your quality of mind when you return to your breath. Are you angry? Are you judging yourself? Are you calm and peaceful? Our aim is to notice, and to encourage ourselves to accept our wandering minds and return to our breathing as peacefully as we can. Don't pretend to be peaceful if you aren't. Simply be as aware as you can be.

Now what do we do? For this week, we just stay present with our breathing. We continue to focus our attention on our breathing in the abdomen, and we become aware of just how our breath is in our belly. Is it deep or shallow? Is it short or long? We see whether our simple awareness of our breathing, and the feelings that come up, changes or shifts as we continue to observe it. Perhaps the shallow and rapid breathing becomes deeper and slower as we continue our sitting meditation. Now what thoughts or feelings go along with our deep and slow breathing? Again, once we've asked the question, the answer is clear and obvious. Try this exercise and see what happens!

Where We Sit

When I first started Zen practice, I practiced at the Cambridge Zen Center, an urban meditation center on a side street near a busy part of town. At least one window of the meditation hall was always open when we did sitting meditation, in freezing winter or sultry summer. We were treated routinely to the sounds of automobiles, honking horns, conversations of passing pedestrians, and police and fire sirens. At first I thought these were awful distractions from my sitting. As I became more grounded in the practice, I realized that these sounds were part of everyday life, and that if I were to wake up to the present moment, the moment would include those sounds. I now prefer to do sitting meditation in a room with lots of natural light and open windows.

It is important not to close off all of our senses when we do sitting meditation. Some seclusion is helpful: We want to sit in a serene environment with minimal distractions if we can. To be serene, however, does not mean that we have to divorce ourselves from the world around us. You will see as we progress that part of what happens in mindfulness practice is the dissolution of the barrier between inside and outside. The practice of mindfulness encourages us to do it right in the world in which we live — whether in sitting meditation, walking meditation, or daily-life mindfulness.

WALKING MEDITATION

Walking meditation is meditation in motion. By walking slowly and being aware of our breath, we have the chance to come in contact with how our bodies move when we walk and to see the world around us with unhurried attention.

We approach this walking as a pure mindfulness activity. This is walking for the sake of walking, without any destination or goal. This is aimless, but not pointless; it is very focused and concentrated. We walk each footstep by itself, not paying attention to the one before it or anticipating the one to come. We walk with awareness of what is inside us and around us. We walk with such careful attention that we become aware, as Thich Nhat Hanh has put it, that walking on the earth is a miracle. Taking just a few steps this way can free us from striving. Walking this way for even ten minutes can refresh us for hours.

There are two kinds of walking meditation. The first is called "slow walking" (sometimes called *kinhin*). In kinhin, our concentration is primarily on the body's activity of walking: the movement of our breath, the motion of our legs and feet, the shifts in our balance and weight, and so on. When we do kinhin walking, we keep our eyes focused on the floor at about a 45-degree angle. This focus helps us to keep our attention inside ourselves and be free of distractions. Most people find it helpful to keep their hands clasped in front of their abdomen, which helps with balance. We walk slowly, taking one step to our in-breath and one step to our out-breath. With each breath, we are aware of the movement of our breathing and of the movement of our feet and legs. We can become aware of our foot lifting off the ground, of the shift of our weight to the other leg, of our foot then making contact with the ground. We can be aware, too, of our mind's activities, and refocus our attention on our breath and our steps.

To practice this kind of walking meditation at home is very helpful, perhaps after you've done some sitting meditation. It is also a nourishing practice to do with others. If you and some friends get together for sitting meditation, try some kinhin meditation as well. When we walk single file as a group, as we do in class, we can see that each one of us is part of something larger — a line of people walking together. This is one simple way to break the illusion that we are separate from one another.

Another type of walking meditation, which we can do anywhere, is designed to help us to be in touch with the refreshing things in the world. As you can imagine, we walk a little faster in this version. This walking meditation practice comes to us from Vietnam. Originally designed to be done outdoors, it is intended to enhance our awareness of where we are and what we are doing, like any mindfulness meditation. To differentiate between this type of walking meditation and the slower version, we will call the slower version by its Asian name *kinhin*, and this faster version by the name *walking meditation*.

In walking meditation, we pay the same attention to our legs, feet, breath, and so on as we do in kinhin, but we walk at a leisurely stroll: perhaps two or three steps for each in-breath and two or three steps for each out-breath. We keep our attention inside, and at the same time we look around and allow ourselves to be aware of the wonders that surround us: the sky, the buds on the trees, the scent of flowers, the sound of a boat on the river. We can do this kind of walking anywhere: on the riverbank, from the subway to the door of our home, from our desk to the bathroom and back. Even if we have a destination, we still do our best to walk as though our only "goal" is that of taking the step we are taking right now.

As we walk, we may see, hear, or smell something that we want to savor. When we do, we stop, breathe in and out several times, and enjoy what we encounter. We breathe to be fully present. This helps us to more fully enjoy whatever we are stopping to admire, just as it helps us enjoy our mindful steps. Then we go on. In this way our walking can be relaxed and enjoyable. If it is not, then we're probably doing something wrong, such as trying too hard. Adjust your pace so that you feel relaxed and comfortable. Don't be surprised if you slow down some the more you do it!

It is helpful to set aside some time every day to do walking meditation just for itself. If you have time just before lunch, that is ideal. Walking meditation in the middle of the workday can make the afternoon much easier. But we can practice walking meditation any time. We can do it when walking from our desk to the bathroom at work, when going out to get lunch, when walking from our house to the subway or bus. Even if you are walking somewhere, such as toward your car, or to the house or the bathroom, please do your best to walk as though you didn't have to arrive anywhere. Walking for the sake of walking, each step for the sake of each step, is very important.

Some people like to count their steps as a way to reinforce their concentration on their walking by saying silently, "One, two, three" on the in-breath and "One, two, three" on the out-breath to correspond with their steps. Some people just prefer to be aware of their breathing and stepping. And some prefer to use gathas, those little poems that set a tone and direction.

Whether you are doing kinhin or walking meditation, please allow yourself to become aware of the quality of the contact your feet make with the ground. Do you walk gently on the earth, taking steps of peace? Are your steps hard and heavy? Your steps will reflect your state of mind — angry steps, calm steps, fearful steps, loving steps — and here the miracle of mindfulness becomes clearly apparent. You will find that as you allow yourself to become truly mindful and aware of your walking — of your feet making contact with the earth, of the motion of the bones and muscles in your feet and legs, of the shift of your body's weight — you will become more relaxed and your steps gentler. Or as one mindfulness practitioner once put it, "My feet love the floor."

Walking meditation can also be a powerful way to bear witness to difficult situations. Some of us hold walking meditation vigils to bear witness to those who die in wars or in urban violence. Zen teachers Bernard Tetsugen Glassman and Claude AnShin Thomas lead walking meditations in concentration camp sites in Europe. In your own life, doing walking meditation with focus, stability, and openness can help you be in touch with suffering in a calm and peaceful way. If you feel awful, take your awfulness for a walk. Breathe and step. Be aware of your feelings and of what surrounds you. If you know someone in trouble, walk for them. Your walk is an offering of love and support.

When I began doing kinhin meditation, I did it in meditation centers where we took our shoes off and sat and walked barefoot or in socks. I have falling arches and my feet pronate. I wear arch supports in my shoes, so walking barefoot is difficult for me. Even today, when I do kinhin, I am very aware of how my foot makes contact with the floor, how my foot and ankle move around to find some balance, how my arch tends to collapse and my leg falls inward. Kinhin and outdoor walking meditation have made me far more aware of how I walk, and as a result I walk better and more securely. When I first started doing kinhin, keeping my balance was very difficult for me because of my feet. Now it is easier, and I can actually help my muscles hold my arch up when I put my weight on my foot. Walking meditation has become one of my favorite practices. Wherever you start with walking meditation, the practice can help you, too.

Here are a couple of gathas for walking meditation. You can say these gathas to yourself silently as you walk. Each line of the poem has a handy "key word." The key word is in parentheses at the end of each line. As you breathe in and take your steps, you can say the key word of the first line; as you breathe out and take your steps, you can say the key word of the second line; and so on to the end of the gatha. If you like the gatha, you can repeat it as many times as you wish; or you may wish to use it once and let it go, and just be with your awareness of your breath and your steps. The first gatha is by Thich Nhat Hanh. The second comes to us from the Japanese and Vietnamese Zen traditions.

I have arrived,	ARRIVE
I am home	HOME
In the here	HERE
And the now.	NOW
I am solid,	SOLID
I am free.	FREE
In the ultimate	ULTIMATE
I dwell.	DWELL

My mind can go in a
          thousand directions.   MIND
Now I walk in peace.   PEACE
Each step creates a warm breeze.   BREEZE
With each step, a lotus blooms.   BLOOM

If you want more guidance and encouragement in this wonderful practice, read Thich Nhat Hanh's *The Long Road Leads to Joy* listed in the recommended reading list.

WHAT COMES UP

"I Can't Find the Time to Do Sitting Meditation"

By the beginning of the second week of practice, most people in my meditation classes are working on establishing a regular sitting meditation practice and are encountering obstacles. Please don't get discouraged if you find it difficult to arrange the time for sitting practice, or if you find it difficult to remember to do your daily-life mindfulness activity. You're in good company!

The secret here is something called "habit energy." As we live our lives, we get into the habit of doing certain things in certain ways. We follow our personal habits when we go to bed at night, when we get up in the morning, when we eat, as we brush our teeth, and when we prepare to deal with good or challenging life situations. Although we learn some of these habits later in life, most are ones we acquired in childhood, often from our parents and teachers. Most of us are unconscious of these habits; after all, our actions become a matter of habit when they are so familiar to us that we perform them without conscious thought. We just see them as normal behavior.

These habits create inertia against change. When left to our unconscious devices, we'll perform them over and over again until we encounter something that tells us not to. Have you ever tried to break a habit? Perhaps you were a smoker, or perhaps you had a habit of going to bed late when you were younger. Do you remember how difficult it was to break those habits?

Habits that have been with us the longest generate the strongest habit energy. We have to call on powerful resources to counter that habit energy. Mindfulness practice is one powerful resource. At first, using mindfulness practice to change our habit energy is like planting a toothpick in a railway track to stop a runaway freight train. The toothpick doesn't stand a chance. Every time we practice mindfulness, however, we nourish the toothpick and help it to grow into a mighty tree. The more we nourish mindfulness, the less we nourish our habits, and the freight train begins to slow down. Eventually, the tree will stop the train.

When we begin doing sitting meditation and daily-life mindfulness practice, most of us are going against the deeply entrenched habit of being unconscious of what we are doing and of our breathing. We are also trying to change our habits in our daily routine when we introduce sitting meditation. We need to make time for it, and for most of us, doing that means rearranging our schedule.

If you forget your daily-life mindfulness activity one day, then do your best the next day. If you have problems finding a time to do sitting meditation, try sitting for ten minutes after you wake up in the morning.

"*I Keep Forgetting...*"

Even if the things we are introducing into our lives are beneficial and enjoyable, as mindfulness practice and sitting meditation are, breaking habit energy requires dedication and diligence. Please don't think you are the only one who says in frustration:

"I keep forgetting my breathing during sitting meditation."

"I keep forgetting my daily-life mindfulness activity."

"I can't meditate."

Just about everyone who starts the practice finds these issues coming up in some form or other. Those of us who are perfectionists, or those of us who get discouraged quickly, find that these issues come up more forcibly.

So please do not give in to your discouragement. Each moment is an opportunity to begin again. These are not just tired old watchwords. Sometimes, when I sit down to do sitting meditation, everything flows smoothly. Sometimes, though, it's a complete mess. Some days I can remember to be mindful more moments than not; other days I wake up somewhere in the afternoon and wonder how I got there. We do not progress in this practice in a straight line. We do well and we do not so well. What I've learned is that the messy days are at least as fruitful as the easy ones, if not more so. They are less comfortable, but I learn a lot from them. The good news is that it gets better as we go along...

So please be easy on yourself. You aren't alone, and you have not failed.

Home Play

FORMAL PRACTICE: Try to increase your sitting meditation time by five or ten minutes each day. Try to begin each sitting period by counting your breaths, and then begin focusing on the turning point of your breathing and on the quality of your breathing. Finish each sitting practice period with a few minutes of kinhin walking.

INFORMAL PRACTICE: Keep doing your daily-life mindfulness activity from last week, and try to add another one from the list in the "First Week" section of this book. If you have a watch with a "beep-beep" hourly alarm, stop each time the alarm goes off and breathe in and out three times. Try to do walking meditation whenever you go to the bathroom.

Increasing Awareness

What to Do with Thoughts and Feelings

Larry Rosenberg, a veteran insight meditation teacher, likes to say, "*When* your mind wanders…notice I said 'when', not 'if.'" Thoughts and feelings arise naturally during sitting meditation. Please don't think there's something wrong with you when they do!

Our mind's job is to think, like our lungs' job is to breathe. Like our breath, our thoughts and feelings come and go. Our in-breath rises, and our out-breath passes away. In the same way, our thoughts and feelings arise and pass away. Even the stubborn ones that seem to be cast in concrete do arise and pass away. Just to realize that simple fact is, for many of us, a major, liberating step. It is our first inkling that reality is not what we think.

We want to hold awareness of our breathing, our thoughts, and our feelings together in the stable light of mindfulness. Our capacity to do this is usually minimal at first and increases with practice, so we begin by focusing our attention first and foremost on our breath. Last week, when your mind wandered, you perceived that you were thinking, and you returned your attention to your breath. This week, when thoughts or feelings arise, you may want to name them so you can identify them as, for example, "anger" or "happiness" or " frustration." This naming may encourage you to remain conscious and aware of your mind's activities. After you have named the thought or the feeling, you can return to your breathing until the next one comes up, and then repeat the process.

Eventually the naming will fall away, and you will just be present, concentrated, increasingly aware of what is going on. Your awareness will encompass the reality of the thought or feeling, beyond the concepts or labels you might be tempted to put on it.

One meditation teacher invites us to envision the true nature of our mind as a clear blue sky. Thoughts, feelings, sensations, and perceptions are clouds that come and go across the blue sky. Some clouds are white wisps, others dark gray thunderheads. Sometimes the clouds are few; sometimes they reach from horizon to horizon. Yet, however many clouds may obscure the blue sky, the blue sky is always there. Just as a small patch of blue often appears during a hurricane, the blue-sky true nature of our mind/heart can reveal itself through the clouds of thinking, feeling, and perceiving, no matter how dense they become.

We all suffer from fear and other forms of ill-being. These will surface in sitting meditation just as they surface in the rest of our lives. Most of us wish to avoid them, and therefore they pose special problems to us as we practice mindfulness meditation. Yet these difficult or painful thoughts or feelings also provide us with our most powerful door to healing and transformation. We don't want to throw our suffering out. We want to wake up. If we let ourselves look deeply into our suffering and allow the true nature of our anger or fear to reveal itself to us in a non-analytical, spontaneous way, we create the possibility of healing and true joy.

Healing doesn't necessarily banish the difficult thoughts or feelings forever. The more chronic ones may still exist in some form. Mindfulness heals them by changing our relationship to them. We will explore this in more detail later. For now, let's just allow the difficult thoughts and feelings to be there. Let's hold ourselves present with them by not pushing them away. We can treat difficult thoughts or feelings in an ordinary way, and we can name them. Naming the thoughts or feelings makes them smaller. If we say to ourselves, "Hello, my [anger, fear, anxiety, worry, or other emotion]. I know that you are part of me. Let's go for a walk," the battle inside us will start to subside. We may not use those words, but that welcoming attitude is essential.

To practice the art of mindfulness means to come to rest in the present moment, with whatever is here, whether it happens to be our pain or our joy. Coming to rest means that we allow our minds to settle right here and now, and that we become aware of how our discursive thinking helps us to hide from what we don't want to face. When we want only happiness, our suffering is intolerable. We'll do anything not to face it, even if we have to create elaborate labyrinths of thoughts to distract us. Similarly, when we are addicted to suffering, we create elaborate narratives to keep ourselves in pain so that we don't have to admit the possibility that we could be happy. Either way, we are running from our own truth: We have suffering and we have joy. That is our basic human condition. It doesn't always have to be this way, but we have to face our suffering before we can heal it.

To practice mindfulness meditation and to live a mindful life, we must first open ourselves to the realization that we try our best to hide. A feeling arises — terror, say — and instead of living with it we create a whole tapestry of thoughts about it. That's hiding. Our prolific minds keep creating diversions for us. When we are stuck in our suffering, we are still lost in our concepts, as in this case, the concept of the story of our life. All we do is recite the story over and over again. So how do we come to rest? We cultivate mindfulness of breathing. We become aware of our breath, we enter into the present moment, and we stop. Then we have the opportunity to recognize our thinking and identify our thought or feeling. Being aware of our difficult thoughts and feelings in this way is not the same as being stuck in our suffering. We can do this anytime, anywhere, not just during formal sitting meditation. Try some abdominal breathing, restore your stability and mindfulness, and then allow the difficult thought or feeling to reemerge. Your relationship to it will already have changed.

To allow ourselves to come to rest and to handle these self-constructed narratives of our lives with true mindfulness requires some trust. We have to trust that simply returning to the awareness of our breathing will take us out of the loop without suppressing our feelings. You will need to try this and experience it within yourself before you will really know that this can happen.

Awareness of the Body

One of the most direct ways we can translate mindfulness into our daily lives is to become aware of what our body is doing while it is doing it. This may sound easy and obvious; after all, aren't we all aware of what our body is doing?

Some years ago I was asked to work with a ballet dancer who was experiencing asthma attacks before and during performances. I had assumed that a dancer would be very much "in" her body while she was dancing, very aware of each body movement while it was happening. As I talked with this ballerina, I found the opposite to be true. As she danced, she had her mind planning the actions she would be making two or three movements from where she was. Her mind was never in contact with what her body was doing while she was doing it. If a professional athlete like a dancer is not aware of what her body is doing while she is doing it, how much less likely are the rest of us to have that awareness?

Stop and consider for a moment: What are your hands doing right now? Are you perhaps tapping your foot? What position are your legs in? How are you holding your head? While you are reading this, stop for a moment and become aware deeply of the position of your body. Allow your mindful breathing to be your anchor as you bring your awareness back home into your body. How am I holding my back? Where are my feet? Is there tension in my jaw? As you explore each of these areas of your body, you can become aware of how your breath seems to enter that part of your body. We will explore this mindfulness of our bodies in a more complete and structured fashion in the fifth week. For now, simply being aware of where you and your body are in space is all that's important.

Now, put down this book and stand up. As you do this, allow yourself to become aware of how your body changes as you move from a sitting to a standing position. The positions of the bones, ligaments, muscles, and tendons are all different. Now consider how many times you stand up and sit down every day. Perhaps you can try to use this kind of body awareness with your standing up and sitting down. You might use it as a bell of mindfulness, to remind you to be aware. Start by using your conscious breathing to bring you into the present moment. Two or three breaths should be enough. Then sit or stand slowly enough so that you can experience the movement of your muscles and bones. You can also make this body awareness part of getting into and out of bed every day, and thus become aware of the difference in your body as it stands, sits, and lies down.

This practice integrates well with walking meditation. Both of them increase our body awareness and bring us back into the present moment. Both encourage mindfulness, or rather, are direct enactments of mindfulness itself. They are easy to incorporate into our daily lives. I hope you enjoy your mindful sitting, standing, walking, and lying down.

Mindfulness Gathas

As I mentioned before, gathas are small poems designed to help us in meditation practice, whether we are sitting, walking, or slicing potatoes. A gatha accomplishes several aims: It occupies our thinking; it sets a direction for our practice at that moment; and, if used correctly, it helps us to be mindful of our breathing.

To understand how gathas occupy our thinking, consider this story. A man walking down the road one day saw another man with a genie. The man was intrigued and asked if perhaps the genie were available. The other replied that he would give the man the genie, but warned him: "The genie will do anything you want, but once you run out of things for it to do it will destroy you." The man thought nothing of this; after all, he had so much the genie could do! He prepared his list and the genie went off happily and did it all. After a while, the lists got shorter and shorter, and the man could not think of more things for the genie to do. He remembered the admonition and became frightened that the genie would destroy him, so he went to his local meditation teacher and asked, "What can I do?" The teacher responded, "Tell the genie to build a pole in the backyard, and then to run up and down it." So the man told the genie to build the pole, and to this day the genie is happily running up and down.

In this story, the genie is our thinking mind, and the pole is a gatha. The gatha occupies our mind and gives it focus. Unlike a mantra, which is the same for all occasions, we can have specific gathas for specific activities. We can have gathas for waking up in the morning, for turning on the light, for using the toilet, for turning on the television, for answering the telephone, for driving the car. The list of gathas can be as long as there are activities. For example, here is a gatha for driving a car:

This car is my legs.
It goes where I choose.
When I drive with awareness,
Everyone lives in safety.

If we use this gatha when we get into the car or while we are driving it, we will have an aid to keep our attention on our driving. The gatha also directs our attention toward the interbeing nature of ourselves and the car ("This car is my legs"). Each gatha encourages mindfulness and also seeks to awaken us to the true nature of the world as it is contained in that action.

Gathas are best used in coordination with our breath. As we breathe in, we can say the first line to ourselves; as we breathe out, the second line; and so forth. In this way, we touch the act we are performing with the gatha, and we touch our breathing too. As we become more grounded in our breathing, mindfulness of breathing will assist mindfulness of the action, and so breathing, action, and gatha go together. Each reinforces the other, and our ability to be in the moment is increased.

Some people find it difficult to remember an entire gatha. It may be easier and simpler to remember one or two key words from each line, words that will remind you of the rest of the line. For example, here is a gatha for sitting meditation:

Sitting in the present moment,
I breathe mindfully.
Each in-breath nourishes love,
each out-breath, compassion.

Here the key words could be *present moment, mindfully, love,* and *compassion.*

What do you do if you are breathing in and you feel anything but love, or your mind is running riot? When using gathas, encourage your true feelings to surface rather than suppressing them. For example, you might be *saying,* "Each in-breath nourishes love" but *thinking,* "It certainly does not. I'm tired and miserable!" The gatha is doing its work, pointing you in the direction of being more loving and compassionate to your aching back while you allow your feelings and thoughts to arise by being fully present. Go back to the section "What to Do with Thoughts and Feelings" for more guidance.

Here are some gathas for daily use. Notice how each gatha sets a direction for mindfulness. You can make up your own for any activity of which you particularly want to be mindful during your day.

WAKING UP

As I wake up, I welcome a new day,
A mindful smile with every breath.
May I live each moment
With compassion and awareness.

FIRST STEPS OF THE DAY

As I take my first step,
My foot kisses the floor.
With gratitude to the earth,
I walk in liberation.

TURNING ON THE WATER

As I turn on the water,
My body's essence pours before me.
Clouds, oceans, rivers, and deep wells
All support my life.

WASHING DISHES

Each dish I wash
Is my most cherished child.
Each movement contains
Boundless love.

FLUSHING THE TOILET

My body's waste is compost.
Down the hopper it goes,
Returning to the earth.

WALKING MEDITATION

My mind can go in a thousand directions.
Now I walk in peace.
Each step creates a warm breeze.
With each step, a lotus blooms.

SITTING DOWN FOR MEDITATION

Sitting in the present moment,
I breathe mindfully.
Each in-breath nourishes love,
Each out-breath, compassion.

SITTING MEDITATION

Each thought, each feeling
Creates the world.
I hold joy and suffering
Tenderly in each breath.

CALMING THE MIND

Chasing after the world
Brings chaos.
Allowing it all to come to me
Brings peace.

TURNING ON THE TELEVISION

Mind and television
Receive what I choose.
I select well-being
And nourish joy.

DRIVING THE CAR

This machine is my legs.
It goes where I choose.
When I drive with awareness,
everyone lives in safety.

PREPARING FOOD

Earth, water, sun, and air,
All live in this food I prepare.

TURNING ON AN ELECTRIC LIGHT

Ancient trees, water, and wind
Join my hand to bring light
To this moment.

HUGGING

I am so happy to hug my dear _____ .
I know (s)he is real in my arms.

PROBLEMS AT WORK

When things fall apart on the job
I vow with all beings
To use this regretful energy
And pick up the pieces with care.

GOING TO SLEEP

Falling asleep at last
I vow with all beings
To enjoy the dark and the silence
And rest in the vast unknown.

HOME PLAY

FORMAL PRACTICE: Try to find a time during the middle of your day to do walking meditation, preferably out-doors. In your sitting meditation, continue to begin each sitting by counting your breaths. Then continue by noticing the turning point of your breathing, the quality of your breath, and the thoughts and feelings that come up. Try naming the thoughts and feelings as they arise. Be aware of your body movements as you sit down for sitting meditation and as you stand up afterward. If you move any part of your body during sitting meditation, try to do it slowly and with complete awareness of each aspect of the movement while it is happening.

INFORMAL PRACTICE: Add another daily-life mindfulness activity from the list, so that you are now doing three. Try doing at least one of these activities using a gatha to help you focus your attention. Keep listening to your watch alarm. Do walking meditation from your house to your car, bicycle, or public transit. Find one activity during the day that calls upon you to change your body position, either standing, sitting, or lying down, and practice body awareness.

FOURTH WEEK

Who Am I?

In this chapter, we explore a practice that reinforces our innate ability to look at ourselves clearly. How we understand ourselves and our world grows out of our concepts and our culture, including the language we speak and our upbringing — everything, in short, that forms our identity. We begin to peer around these concepts as we practice awareness of our thoughts and feelings, and this frees us so that we can make different choices. Now we begin to glimpse who we really are and what the world really is. For an instant, we throw away our concepts and ideas and we embody our luminous True Nature. How do we deepen this awareness?

Who Am I? What Is This?

The late Mu Deung Sunim (Zen Master Su Bong), my first Zen teacher, used to tell this story:

When Mu Deung first started practicing mindfulness, he heard that in the old days a great Zen master in China had attained enlightenment as he was passing through the public market when he happened to hear someone recite a line from the Diamond Sutra, a great Buddhist text. "If it worked for that old Zen master," Mu Deung thought, "it will work for me." He found a copy of the Diamond Sutra, located the line that the old Zen master had heard, and read it. Nothing happened. He read it again. Still nothing happened. He was baffled. He went to see his teacher, Zen Master Seung Sahn. Perhaps, he thought, if Seung Sahn reads the line to me, or at least explains it, the magic would happen.

Mu Deung knocked on Seung Sahn's door. Seung Sahn was sitting in his room watching old cowboy movies on television, which he did to improve his English.

"Yes?" said the Zen master.

Mu Deung said, "I read the line in the Diamond Sutra that gave the Sixth Patriarch enlightenment, and nothing happened. Can you help me?"

Seung Sahn motioned Mu Deung to sit opposite him at a low table. "Show me the line," he said.

As soon as Mu Deung started to read him the line, Seung Sahn interrupted him. "No, show me," he said.

Mu Deung thought, "He must be really stupid." He turned the book to face Seung Sahn and put his finger on the page, pointing to the line.

In one swift motion, Seung Sahn slammed the book closed on Mu Deung's finger, and pulled him toward him. They faced each other, eye to eye, across the table.

"WHO ARE YOU?!?!?!" the teacher shouted.

Mu Deung was stunned. He could not answer. Seung Sahn let go of the book, pulled back slightly, and said again, quietly and gently, "Who are you?" Mu Deung then realized that he had no answer to that question. He had no idea who he was.

Seung Sahn was pointing out to Mu Deung that he had to develop insight by examining himself and the world directly, but that layers of concepts and assumptions blocked the way. We are all like Mu Deung. If we ask ourselves the question "Who am I?" and if we are honest, we will acknowledge that we haven't the slightest idea. All of our answers to that question are tags and labels. We say we are Christian or Jewish, a man or a woman, white or brown or black, old or young, but none of these answers tells us who we really are. All they tell us is how we have chosen to identify ourselves. They are mental constructs, but what do they have to do with the deeper reality of our own being? Take away the words and labels, and then let me know who you are. Can you do this? At a deep, fundamental level, who we are is a great mystery. Even if we say, "I am a human being," do we have any idea what a human being is? Again, if we are honest, we will answer that we don't have a clue.

And, if we don't know who we are, how can we know what anything else is? Do we really know what a faucet is? Take away the label: Remove the word *faucet,* and then let me know what a faucet is.

Do you know who your spouse, partner, parent, or child is? Please be honest. Our perceptions of each other are filtered through our own ideas and emotions, and to some extent they are all flawed. What would it be like, for one moment, to drop your assumptions about the most important person in your life? If we have no idea who those closest to us are, how can we know with clarity about our neighbors, our community, our country, or the world? Can you see how important this question is, and how naturally it flows out of and back into the quality of mindfulness we are trying to cultivate?

When we ask this question, the question itself is important, and not the answer. We are encouraged to ask, "Who am I?" or "What is this?" and to answer, "I don't know." The question and answer become a powerful way to liberate ourselves from the mental constructs that we put on the world every moment of every day. In my classes, some students find that asking, "Who am I?" and answering, "I don't know," makes them profoundly uncomfortable. This kind of direct challenge to the deepest convictions we hold about who and what we are is unsettling. It puts us at the edge of the cliff. Be aware of your discomfort. I encourage you to say "I don't know" even if you squirm. In my experience, that answer really does short-circuit our labels and constructs and can give us, even if just for one moment, a direct, unvarnished encounter with the present moment.

This is not a game. It is a direct way to allow us to experience life without the usual ideas and concepts standing in the way. It provides a clear, unequivocal direction for our practice. One friend of mine refers to this as "the graceful state of not knowing." As we go through our daily-life mindfulness activities, this state can help us a great deal if we have the willingness to ask, when we turn on the electric light, "What is this?" and the courage to answer, "I don't know." When Seung Sahn asks one of his students a question and the student answers, "I don't know," he likes to say, "Just keep this 'don't know' mind — no problem."

Zen Master Bo Mun exhorts his students never to settle for the answer they already know. If we truly don't know, if we keep ourselves truly open and free of concepts and ideas, we can approach each moment of our lives with freshness. We can see what is happening in the present moment without assumptions about the past or ideas about the future. Yes, it is frightening to cut ourselves loose from our moorings that way. It is also the door to freedom.

We can bring this practice into the mindfulness of breathing that we have nurtured over these past weeks. We continue to be aware of the quality of our breath and use these questions, "Who am I? What is this?" in conjunction with our awareness of breathing to help deepen our practice. To do this, allow yourself to be as aware as you can during your sitting that you don't know what breathing really is. What is an in-breath? For one moment, assume that you don't know. Take one in-breath with that assumption. Just allow yourself to be present with that in-breath, with the pause between the in-breath and the out-breath, with the next out-breath, and hold the realization that you don't know what breathing is, or what not-breathing is. For many of us, developing this "don't know" practice is both frightening and liberating: frightening because we are attached to our assumptions about life, and liberating because we can feel the freshness and freedom that come with dropping those assumptions.

We can apply this practice to our walking meditation, eating meditation, and daily-life mindfulness practices. Try walking with the question "What is this?" about your foot and the ground. Just before you put a bite of food in your mouth, try asking the question "What is this?" For those who have difficulties using gathas, this "don't know" practice can be an alternative to gathas for daily-life mindfulness. Both lead us to the same point, but where the gatha gives us a beautiful path, the "Who am I? What is this?" questions put us on the edge of a cliff. Which do you prefer? Perhaps a bit of both can be helpful. Or perhaps you can combine them by taking those "Who am I? What is this?" questions and keeping them in the background of your awareness while you use the gatha.

We can deepen every moment of our day, whether we are doing the informal practice of daily-life mindfulness or the formal practices of sitting and walking meditation, by breathing in with the questions: "Who am I? What is this?" and then breathing out, gratefully, with this answer: "I don't know." Let's bring this great question into our mindfulness of daily life.

MAKING CHOICES
(WHAT TO DO WITH THOUGHTS
AND FEELINGS, CONTINUED)

Many of my students, at this point in the course, are disturbed that they cannot stop themselves from thinking. They tell me that they are caught up in their thinking, find this very uncomfortable, and figure that the way out is to stop their minds from thinking. In my experience, that's impossible: Our mind's job is to think, just as our eye's job is to see or our stomach's job is to digest food. But the pain is very real. This is an important stage in the development of our practice. At this point we begin to realize how we let ourselves get trapped in our minds and just how mindfulness can help us find a way out. This is where we begin to see that practice is not about doing what's comfortable; it's about doing what's necessary.

When we say that we are caught up in our thinking, we are really saying that we are attached to our narrative. The narrative is the story we tell ourselves about our lives: all the reasons we are the way we are, all the reasons why things happen to us. Our attachment to the narrative keeps us powerless. The narrative's job is to remind us that we are subject to forces we cannot control — other people, heredity, social problems, and of course, our habits and feelings. Our attachment to the narrative keeps us in the role of victim. The reason for this is simple: The narrative is the intellectualization of our emotions. It is also the creator, and the result, of our habits. It doesn't let us understand that we can choose how to face our feelings or that we can decide whether or not to follow our habits. Once we are locked into the narrative, we think and act out our lifetime's patterns of behavior.

One way to disengage from the narrative is to foster an appreciation of our minds. In the Buddhist world, the mind is considered a sense organ, just like the eyes, ears, nose, tongue, and skin. Just as sight is the activity of the eye, thinking is an activity of the mind. Like our eyes, the mind is active in doing its job: It creates an endless succession of thoughts and perceptions. Sometimes, however, the mind, like our eyes or other senses, does not "see" everything. Just as some things in the world are beyond the field of our vision, so does the present moment hold more than the thoughts presently in our awareness.

This approach works on changing our attitude: Instead of being caught up in the drama of the narrative and believing that everything we think is the only truth, we start to cultivate wonder instead at the fecundity of this sense organ, the mind. This becomes a way to disengage from the drama and to take the narrative with a grain of salt. We can foster this appreciation by considering how helpful the mind can be in many situations in our lives, how it helps us balance a checkbook or drive a car or parse a sentence. We can appreciate our minds for what they do in the same way that we appreciate our eyes for what they do.

At the same time, we couple that appreciation of the mind with our awareness that we are in fact more than what we are thinking at this particular moment. Our bodies, or a sound, may enter into our awareness and share the space with our thinking. Allowing ourselves to be aware of something outside ourselves — a tree, or the blue (or cloudy) sky, a flower, or anything else we enjoy — can also foster this awareness. I find that walking meditation works particularly well for me in this practice. When I walk, I focus on my breathing and my steps, and this puts me in touch with something other than my thinking, even while my mind rambles. Gradually my horizon widens, my attention broadens, and I can thank my mind for what it is trying to do, as well as acknowledge that what my mind is doing right now is not helping me very much. Sometimes, when I get caught up in my narrative, I don't have the opportunity to do walking meditation, and then I will simply focus on my breath and allow myself to notice the sounds in my environment. I invite the sounds into my awareness, so that the sounds are happening inside of me rather than outside. You can experiment to find the approach to this practice that works for you.

As we continue to practice and become stabler, we begin to experience a spaciousness opening inside us. One Zen teacher, Mel Ash, refers to this as "shaving the inside of your skull." I usually refer to it as the space around our thoughts. As this happens, we begin to disengage from the narrative. As we grow stabler in our mindful breathing, we experience more spaciousness around our thoughts. In this spaciousness, our experience of the natural process of thinking and feeling expands. We see thoughts and feelings arise and pass away. The more we see the impermanence of thoughts and feelings, the more we experience the reality of the mind as a sense organ, and we feel less trapped. My experience is this: When I feel space around a thought, then I also feel that something else is present besides that thought. The "something else" is mindfulness. If something else is present, then the thought is not the only thing I am at that moment. And if I am more than that thought, then that thought no longer has to run me or my life.

This practice helps to calm our minds and stabilize our feelings, and opens us to the possibility of joy in our lives. If we took this approach alone, however, we would probably end up with moments of great delight interspersed with chaos. We would have no real understanding of the thoughts and feelings that would inevitably continue to drive our lives or of how they do that. In the introduction to *A Path with Heart,* Jack Kornfield writes eloquently of the split between spiritual euphoria as a monk in a monastery in Thailand and spiritual confusion in daily life after he returned to the United States and life as a layperson. I had a similar experience. For years I wanted to stay on spiritual retreats because I experienced such great joy there and because the rest of my life continued to be a mess. After I realized that I needed to delve into the pit in which my daily thoughts and feelings were brewing, I began to experience a deeper and more solid joy. As one of Pema Chödrön's meditation students once said, "Joy is about getting real." As soon as you are stabilized and calm, therefore, you need to take another step if you really want to wake up and live an awakened life in this world. That step is to develop the understanding of your own being and the world around you. Once you have done this, you can learn how to put that understanding into action.

To make the step to develop understanding and act on it requires courage. It means acknowledging that you have a choice. If you are aware of a thought that is part of your narrative, and you are aware of an impulse to act that thought out, the next step is to understand that you can choose not to act that way.

Here's an example: During sitting meditation, most of us become preoccupied, at times, with thoughts of what we need to do and feel compelled to get up and do something about it. Taking the next step means

- Being aware of that impulse and not acting on it
- Staying in our "one seat," the seat of practice, and allowing ourselves to be aware of our panic or frustration or whatever we want to call it

- Staying steady with what we are feeling, using our mindful breathing to keep ourselves still in the midst of our raging mental storm

- Acknowledging and identifying what is going on inside of ourselves (naming practice)

- Disengaging from our chattering mental narrative and observing closely our feelings as they arise in our bodies.

Even if all we can do is greet our mental storm with acceptance, we are already doing a lot. The more we do this, the more likely we are to awaken compassion and loving-kindness for ourselves and for the suffering our mind causes us.

In the second part of this book, we will discover four very concrete ways of exploring thoughts and feelings more deeply. At this stage, however, practicing with simple awareness is enough. You can be aware of what comes up during sitting meditation, of your impulse to get up, for example, to move your arm or leg, to scratch your nose or rub your eyes, or to answer the phone when it rings, and resist the impulse to take that action. You can stay steady and experience what happens when you do that. Usually a storm will rage in your mind initially. Just engage in mindful breathing and remain steady with the thoughts and feelings as they rise up and pass away. You will feel the emotions in your body as sensations. Your narrative will then kick in and your mind will create thoughts from these feelings. If you follow the train of your thoughts, you will remove yourself from your feelings and you will spin off into the stratosphere. Identify and acknowledge the thoughts and remain focused on the feelings as much as you can. If you do this, the storm actually abates and you will find yourself sitting more peacefully and steadily than before. You will also have some valuable information about your thoughts and feelings simply by noticing what came up during the storm, acknowledging and accepting it, as well as what came up after the storm, and acknowledging and accepting that as well. Even in acknowledging the pattern of your stormy mind and your more peaceful mind, you will have learned a great deal about how your mind works and how you can choose to create suffering or peacefulness for yourself. You can take this practice into daily life by encouraging yourself to stop and take a "breathing" break when you find yourself becoming reactive: When you feel an uncontrollable impulse to do or say something, that's a good sign to stop, become aware of your breathing, allow the horizon of your awareness to expand, and disengage yourself from your narrative.

As you do this practice, please be patient and kind with yourself. Most of my students expect far too much from themselves early on in the course. Someone with many years of practice might walk steadily through life with the most difficult emotions and the most dreadful thoughts raging in her mind; please do not expect that of yourself. Start where you are: Whatever is coming up, please allow yourself to remain steady with it. Choose to practice and be aware that, if you can choose to practice, you can also choose to act differently in other situations in your life. Whatever situation you are in, you can stop long enough to allow yourself to be steady with what is going on and to understand that you have a choice about what to do or not to do.

EATING MEDITATION

Most of us have developed unhealthy habits around eating. We tend to eat too fast; we watch television or read while we eat; we have distressing conversations. In general, we pay attention to anything else other than the food we put into our bodies. And then we wonder why we get indigestion!

Eating is a wonderful opportunity to practice mindfulness. When we eat mindfully, we can really come in contact with our food. Food is very precious, and not only because we are fortunate to have food to eat. Food gives us the opportunity to see clearly the connection between us and the earth and all of its inhabitants. Every vegetable, every piece of bread, every drop of sauce or mouthful of tea contains in it the life of the planet. Try asking, "What is this?" about your food as you eat it, and really pay attention to what you see, smell, and taste. Bring your mindfulness to bear on a piece of tomato: How many different things can you see in it? Can you see the sun and rain that nourished it, the tomato plant and the soil it grew in, the people who planted it and harvested the tomato, their families and homes, and so on? It is not too extreme to say that the whole universe exists in that piece of tomato. Jesus' offer of bread and wine as his body and blood, at the Last Supper, was quite literal: He was offering the universe in that piece of bread. It's just a change in attitude. Instead of seeing the bread, or the tomato, as something separate from the rest of the world, we see the intimate connection that the food has with everything else. We can eat with that degree of awareness every time; we don't have to wait for a special occasion.

Mindful eating is an ideal opportunity to put the practice of "What is this?" into action. Here are some suggestions for how to do this.

We can engage mindfulness while we prepare the food. Try to peel vegetables, mix sauces, bake bread, cook grains, prepare a casserole, and sauté a meal with mindful attention. Slow down, appreciate the food itself, enjoy the smells and textures and flavors, and make your meal preparation a celebration of life. Ask, "What is this?" about each piece of food you prepare; answer, "I don't know," and see how this affects your appreciation of the food. Try to turn off the radio or television and focus on preparing the food. Ask yourself, "Who am I?" as you prepare your food and answer, "I don't know." Notice your experience of this.

In eating a meal mindfully, we usually spend at least part of the meal, if not all of it, in silence. By eliminating the distraction of conversation, we free more of our attention so we can be mindful of the food in front of us and the process of how we eat. We are thus even more mindful of the friends who are eating with us. We eat slowly enough to be aware of the piece of food we pick up. Notice how you become aware of the aroma, flavor, and texture of each morsel. When you rest your fork or spoon between bites, when you don't put more food in your mouth before you finish chewing and swallowing what you have eaten already, notice how you become aware of each act of eating. Continue your practice of asking "What is this?" about each bite of food.

After the food enters your body, train your mindfulness on your digestion. How does your stomach receive the food? Does it feel tight, or does it relax to accept the food? If your stomach is tight, are you experiencing anxiety or tension? Ask, "What is this?" Answer, "I don't know," and go more deeply into your physical body. If you continue eating with your stomach in this condition, you will be eating your anxiety and tension, not the food. Use mindful awareness to delve into the sensation in your stomach, and see if it relaxes. Then try eating another bite of food: What happens now?

If you want, you can go more deeply into your digestion and become aware of how the food gets broken down in your stomach and intestines, how the nutrients get into your bloodstream, how the cells of your body get nourishment, and how the waste products move through your large intestine and out of your body. Approach your digestive tract as a great mystery to explore. Ask, "What is this?" about your digestion and answer, "I don't know." Let your horizons open up. You can become aware of your body as a great recycling system, and as a part of the cycle of life, just by practicing mindful eating. Please remember that this is not an intellectual, analytical exercise. Let yourself enter into the physical reality of your digestion, not your thoughts about it.

If we eat with a group mindfully, we can use a bell of mindfulness several times during the meal to bring us back to our breath from distraction. We can send a smile of real friendship and deep communication to the others with whom we are eating. If we eat alone, or with others who are not eating mindfully, we can stop every once in a while and look around, breathe, and smile.

At the end of the meal, we can pause to appreciate the food we've eaten. Take a moment to sit quietly and become aware of how your body feels now that your hunger is satisfied. Most of us find that, when we eat mindfully, we eat less. Our food consumption goes down, but our satisfaction goes up. We can then clean up after ourselves. When we wash the dishes and put away the remaining food, we give ourselves the opportunity to appreciate even the plates, silverware, pots, and utensils that have brought the food to us. We can take care of the things that support our eating and, thus, our lives.

You don't have to be eating at home to eat mindfully. I have even done it in fast-food restaurants. It's more challenging, but it's possible and, I find, very helpful. Instead of preparing food mindfully, I appreciate the people who prepare and serve the food. Try this yourself. Be aware of their efforts. Try to address your order taker by name and to treat him or her as your ally in getting your food. When you get your food, go to your table and sit quietly in front of your meal. Try saying the Five Contemplations, which you'll find below, silently to yourself. Then eat your meal mindfully. This is challenging because the atmosphere of most fast-food restaurants is anything but conducive to mindful eating. The constantly playing piped-in music, the activity of other patrons, the bright lighting, and frequently garish colors of the walls, seats, and tables, all contribute to a less-than-serene environment. Slow down, be aware of your breathing, be aware of your food, and be aware of the others around you. Try to smile at the people you see, or at least to look at them directly and acknowledge them as fellow human beings. Eat with awareness of the effort that went into preparing your food; that will help increase your appreciation for the people who work there. At the end of your meal, clean your table thoroughly. You will prepare an attractive space for the next person to use, and you will save the restaurant employees some extra work. All of these activities can increase your enjoyment of eating in challenging surroundings.

Here are some gathas (poems) we can use to help us be mindful of our eating.

FIVE CONTEMPLATIONS BEFORE EATING

This food is the gift of the whole universe — the earth, the sky, and much hard work.
May I be aware of the quality of my deeds as I receive it.
May I practice mindfulness to transform greed, hatred, and ignorance.
May this food nourish me and prevent illness.
In gratitude I accept this food so I may realize the path of love, compassion, and peace.

DRINKING A CUP OF TEA, SODA, WATER, OR ANY LIQUID

This drink is my cup of mindfulness.
I hold the present moment
In my hands.

AFTER THE MEAL

My plate is empty. My hunger is satisfied,
And my body's strength is fully restored.
I use my power for the benefit of all.
May all beings have the nourishment they need.

BEING GROUNDED

In my classes I work extensively with helping my students be grounded. This is important to me because I have spent most of my life being ungrounded and I have seen the difficulties this causes. Most of the people I encounter are also ungrounded, so I see this as a common problem.

By "grounded" I mean having my attention completely and fully inside my body no matter what I'm doing, whether I'm walking the dog or writing this sentence. For years, I perfected being absent from my body. For most of us, lack of groundedness originates in feelings we don't want to acknowledge, and our primary means of escape is into mental activity. Worry, perseveration, rehashing old events, planning multiple scenarios, and replaying our past to remind us of who's responsible for how we feel are all aspects of the mental escape. For me, the predominant feeling is fear. For years, if someone talked to me, I could listen but part of my mind was somewhere else. "Somewhere else" might be worrying about a future activity; it might be rehearsing a conversation I wanted to have with someone else. I could be listening to you and at the same time be on an imaginary podium leading an orchestra in a Beethoven symphony because I was so scared you would "find me out," think me a fraud. Fear so dominated me, and I was so unwilling to let myself feel my fear, that I couldn't really pay attention. Mindfulness practice has allowed me to be grounded in my body most of the time. It can do the same for you.

Think about your life and consider honestly whether you are at home in your body most of the time. Here's a simple and telling example: If you drive, consider whether you have driven somewhere and wondered how you got there. If that has happened to you, you can be guaranteed that during your drive you were nowhere near your body. Do you drop things, or bump into things or people? If you do, chances are you're not grounded.

What's so important about being grounded? If you have followed the progression of exercises in this book, you should see how important it is to pay attention to what you are doing while you are doing it. To accomplish this, you need to be fully in the present moment. To be in the present moment, you must keep your mind in one place and not be drawn away from yourself. When you are drawn away from yourself, you have left your body. When you are completely attentive, you are grounded. As you become more grounded, you may find that you drop things and bump into people and things a lot less often, and you may find that you will remember every moment of your drive from home to work.

The first step in learning to be grounded is to become aware of your breath inside your body. In the first week, you learned to put your hand on your belly to notice the motion of your breathing, the rising and falling of your abdomen. From this beginning, you can allow yourself to become aware of your breath inside your belly, right at your diaphragm. Try letting your attention be on your breath inside your belly as you're reading this. See if you can feel how this draws your attention into your body.

Now, can you be aware of the sounds in your environment? Most of the time we "leave our bodies" to meet the sounds of the world. We hear a birdcall or a car horn, and we perceive the sound as being outside of us. As you continue to breathe and maintain your awareness of your breath on the inside of your belly, see if you can allow the sounds you are hearing right now to come to you. Relax into the breath, and let the sounds be inside you, inside the space between your ears. See if you can expand your hearing, make it inclusive. Try allowing the sounds of the world to come to you.

During your sitting meditation, work on allowing your breath to open a space within your body. As you breathe, let yourself be aware of the space that opens inside your belly with each in-breath. See if you can allow that spaciousness to extend through your entire body: first your chest, then your arms and hands, then your neck and head. Let the spaciousness extend through your belly into your hips and down into your legs and feet. Now, each in-breath opens a space in your entire body. Notice how different this feels. You are grounded in your breath and in your body. You are at home.

In your walking meditation, work on being inside the muscles and joints of your legs as you walk. Really put your attention into your lower limbs. How does your ankle move when you pick up your foot? How does it absorb your weight when you put your foot down? Don't analyze this; simply let yourself be inside of it. If you remember to coordinate your breathing and your steps, try being aware of your breath moving into and through your ankle while you breathe and step. If you can keep your attention in your feet and on your breathing, you are grounded.

In eating meditation, see if you can be aware of the

food moving down your throat and into your stomach. Can you be aware of this from inside your stomach? Use mindful breathing to bring your awareness into your belly and then eat a bite of food. If you can be aware of the food entering your stomach, and how your stomach accepts the food, you are grounded.

In your daily-life mindfulness, use mindful breathing to bring the object of your mindful attention to you. If you are flushing the toilet, try allowing the spaciousness of your breathing to extend down your arm and hand and into the toilet handle. As you breathe, see if you can be aware of the spaciousness of your being encompassing the toilet. Stay grounded in your breath and bring the toilet to you; don't exit your body to meet the toilet. When we do this activity, of course we are not actually bringing these objects into our bodies. We are, instead, making the interconnectedness between ourselves and the objects in our environments something real and tangible. In fact, that toilet is inside me and outside me, both and neither, all at the same time. If this baffles you, don't worry. When you enter deeply into the experience, it will all make sense.

In the meantime, work on keeping yourself grounded. Become aware of the times when you want to escape from your body. We do this when our feelings overwhelm us, or when we find ourselves in situations where we are uncomfortable or feel unsafe. Some of us walk through life overwhelmed by our feelings and spend most of our time outside our bodies. I know this because I've done it. And I know how much difficulty and pain result from it. When you find yourself exiting your body, come back to your breath, bring your breath into your belly, and ground your breath in your body. Let yourself feel the fear, terror, anxiety, worry, despair, or whatever it may be. We experience these feelings in our bodies, not in our rational minds. Observe how your mind spins off into scenarios about your feelings, and step away from the mental activity by returning to your breathing and being aware of the feelings themselves as they live in your body. If you can stay with your feelings in your body, then you are grounded and you are present. Then, you have a chance at life.

And now for a surprise:

In four short weeks, you have learned the very basics of mindfulness practice: how to become aware of your breathing, how to follow your breathing and your actions in everyday life, how to become aware of thoughts and feelings when they arise and how to stay present with them, and how to challenge and begin the process of letting go of your most cherished assumptions about yourself and the world. You now have all the basic tools you need to make mindfulness practice the ground of your life.

If you simply practice mindfulness when you are sitting, walking, standing, lying down, eating, cooking, driving, or doing anything else in your life, your life will change. Living with awareness of what you do and the consequences of your actions will alter your life and your relationships with others. If you follow the practice of asking "Who am I?" and "What is this?" about everything and everyone you encounter, even about every thought and feeling you have — in other words, if you go through life without making any assumptions and simply encounter things as they are — your life will change dramatically. When you live with the awareness that questions are more important than answers, that encountering things as they are is more beneficial than just accepting your old stories about them, a huge burden falls by the wayside and you transform your life.

These practices require meticulous attention. They ask us to pay complete attention to what is happening right now, no more or less. They ask that we live in present time without distraction. They will not allow us to settle for what we already know. Are you ready to change your life?

There is much more to learn and experience. In the next section, we begin to explore the world of our own beings in more detail. We begin to cultivate our awareness of body, feelings and sensations, thinking, and the objects of our mind's focus and attention. So if you think you've reached the end, that's just what you think. The reality is different. Let's go on.

HOME PLAY

FORMAL PRACTICE: Continue to develop your awareness of the quality of your breath and of the thoughts and feelings that arise. See if you can become aware of a space opening inside your breath as you sit. As this space opens, see what happens to your awareness of the sounds in your surroundings. Allow your breathing to lead you into awareness of your thoughts and feelings. See if you can invite your thoughts and feelings into the space within your breath. See if you can hold the question "What is this?" about everything you encounter in your sitting and walking meditation. Do at least part of your sitting practice every day by dropping away any instructions or gathas or guided meditations and focus exclusively on awareness of breathing and the question "What is this?"

INFORMAL PRACTICE: Add another daily-life mindfulness activity from the list, so that you are now doing four. Try to do at least two of these activities using a gatha to help you focus your attention. Eat at least one meal during the week in mindful silence. Do walking meditation and body awareness when you go to the bathroom at work. Do body awareness when you go to bed at night and get up in the morning.

PART TWO

THE FOUR
FOUNDATIONS
OF MINDFULNESS

FIFTH WEEK

Mindfulness
in the Body

In the world of formal mindfulness practice, sitting
meditation has two basic formats. One is what we
might call "open" practice, or simply sitting with what
is. This is the practice we have been learning over the first
four weeks. The other is a guided type of practice. In this
type, we are asked to call deliberately upon certain experiences so that we may examine them more closely. In this
section we will begin to explore guided practice.

Direction or intention in practice is very important.
No matter what type of practice we are doing — formal or
informal, guided or open — we will do it better if we are
aware of why we are practicing. Why are you doing this?
Why are you reading this book? Why do you sit in one
place being aware of your breath and the activities of your
mind? Why do you pause for the telephone and for a red
traffic light? Why, when your mind wanders, do you come
back to awareness of your breathing? Please consider what
your answer is in this moment.

Mindfulness practice is purposeful. It may not have a
goal or a specific end point, but it does have a reason for
being in our lives. Perhaps today your reason for practice

is to relieve mental stress; perhaps tomorrow it will be to get to know your daughter better; perhaps that afternoon you will hear the news and practice because you want to help people and don't know how; perhaps the next day you may practice because you enjoy it; perhaps the day after, or even the next hour, you will practice because life is baffling, you're in emotional pain, and you need stability and insight. This is your direction and intention.

When we do guided practice, the guided meditation sets a direction for us. In open practice, our intention may be as simple as being aware of our breathing and every impression we receive through our senses, or we may use the direction "Who am I?" "What is this?" that we learned in the last chapter. Whatever it may be, our intention in practice will lead us. Let's be as open to what the moment offers us as we can be.

INTRODUCTION OF GATHA-GUIDED MEDITATION

When the Buddha introduced the practice of mindfulness, he suggested that we establish it in four areas: in our bodies, our feelings, our minds, and what he called "objects of mind." The term "objects of mind" refers to anything on which the mind focuses. These four areas are called in the Buddhist tradition the "Four Foundations (or Establishments) of Mindfulness." We will be exploring these four areas through a series of guided meditations.

The tradition of guided meditations in the practice of mindfulness is as old as the Buddha himself. The Buddha used guided meditations as a way of helping people point their practice in a fruitful direction. In one text in particular, "The Full Awareness of Breathing," the Buddha used short poems, gathas, to guide the practice. In our own day, Thich Nhat Hanh has further developed this idea, and the inspiration for the guided meditations in this section come from my experiences with him.

In this form of practice, each part of the meditation is presented as a gatha. As always in our practice using gathas, we coordinate the words of the gatha with the rhythm of our breathing. The full gatha is presented in the left column; key words from the in-breath and out-breath lines of the gatha are presented in the right column. The easiest way to do these gatha-guided meditations is to hold the key words for each stanza in our conscious awareness as we breathe in and out.

Here is a basic guided meditation in gatha form adapted from Thich Nhat Hanh:

(In) I know I am breathing in.	IN
(Out) I know I am breathing out.	OUT
(In) I calm my body and mind.	CALMING
(Out) I smile.	SMILING
(In) I dwell in the present moment.	PRESENT MOMENT
(Out) I know this is a	
* wonderful moment.*	WONDERFUL MOMENT

In the first stanza, we would be aware of *In* on the in-breath and *Out* on the out-breath; in the second stanza, we would be aware of *Calming* on the in-breath and *Smiling* on the out-breath; and so on.

Because we practice mindfulness to awaken us to what is happening in the present moment, we must use the gathas in a way that helps us touch our present reality, not hide from it. For example, when we are practicing with *Calming/Smiling,* we don't want to say "Calming" while we grit our teeth and try to ignore how tense and upset we are. Instead, we want to acknowledge our present situation. So we say, "Calming/Smiling," and inside hear a voice say, "The hell I'm calm, and I'm not smiling at all!" We acknowledge this voice. We don't hide from it, and we don't try to push it away. We say, "Calming," and acknowledge our frazzled nerves at the same time. When we do this well, something wonderful happens: We find ourselves fully aware of our frazzled nerves, and then the frazzling starts to dissipate. After a while we are saying "Calming" and really feeling calm.

So to get to "calm," we need to go through "frazzle." Through it, not around it. We don't want to make the present moment into something other than what it is. Mindfulness practice can heal and transform us, and it does that by putting us directly in touch with our present reality.

Sometimes it isn't helpful to try to work directly with "frazzle." Sometimes we are so out of balance that we get stuck in "frazzle" and don't know how to get out. At times like that, we need to nourish our mindfulness with positive things. Walking meditation outdoors is one of my favorite ways of doing this. Making direct contact with the earth, the sky, the trees, the wind, and the people I see helps me to see that there is more to life than my worries, fears, or pain. We can also nourish our mindfulness by doing anything we truly enjoy, like cooking a meal or working in the garden.

It is important not to hide from "frazzle." We should not use nourishing positive aspects of ourselves as a way to escape from what we are really feeling. We nourish the positive here only to restore balance. Once we have restored our balance, we can return to our "frazzle" — the difficulty we encounter when we point ourselves toward "calm" — and be at one with it in a direct way. Then the healing and transformation can happen naturally. In fact, we may find that "frazzle" comes up while we are doing walking meditation, and suddenly we can embrace it and it can reveal itself to us. This is the backdoor approach. The back door to "frazzle," of course, is "calm." These opposites are just two sides of the same coin. This back-door approach can work as well as the more direct front-door approach, but it requires more care. We must be certain that we are not using the back door as a way of avoiding going through the door at all.

The "guided" part of the guided meditation helps to set a direction for our practice. It sets the direction of calming our body and mind and of acknowledging that any moment when we are alive is a wonderful moment. As we go through our frazzled nerves, and through our feelings of loneliness and despair, that is where we are headed. The guided meditation is a beacon leading us. It may take a while to get there, but the light of the guided meditation is strong. Please trust it. The more you do it, the stronger your practice will become; as your practice grows stronger, your level of calm will be deeper.

Please remember the words of my old teacher Zen Master Seung Sahn: "Don't make anything." What he means is, Don't change the present reality. Encounter it as it is. Please do not use the guided meditation form as a way to avoid. Your breath is as it is right now; please don't try to change it. Your mind is thinking what it is thinking right now; you are feeling what you are feeling right now. Please don't change this. Please use the guided meditation as your North Star to help you to set an intention. Whether you ever get to "calm" is not the point. You will eventually, but don't focus on that; "calm" may not be anything like what you anticipated. What is important is what you encounter on the way. This is your reality, and this is your mind. The focus of practice has not changed; you are still learning about yourself and understanding your mind. It's important to be aware of the tricks your mind plays with the guided meditation form, and believe me, the tricks are there. The one I have most frequently encountered is thinking that I am touching "calm" inside myself, and not understanding that I am *thinking* calm instead of *being* calm. The ways of our mind are subtle; please remember this as you enter into this form of practice.

There will be other gatha-guided meditations later on in this book. In doing any of these meditations, please allow a minimum of five minutes for each segment. Ideally, the first segment should be five minutes, the middle ones should be at least ten minutes each, and the last segment at least another five minutes, although you may enjoy your meditation so much by then that you might want to extend it. If you are sitting in twenty- or thirty-minute cycles, you can expand the meditation over two cycles. And if you wish, you can take any part of the meditation and use it as a direction for an entire sitting meditation period. Please be creative, and at the same time, don't shortchange yourself by giving too little time to each part. If you can, allow yourself to establish stillness in each part of the meditation so that you can really touch that moment.

THE FOUR FOUNDATIONS OF MINDFULNESS

Mindfulness is an embodied practice. *Embodied* means that we experience mindfulness directly and tangibly. When we are truly mindful of our breathing, body and mind touch each other: body because that is where the physical breath occurs, and mind because the breath is where our minds are focused. This kind of mindfulness is spontaneous and unself-conscious. If you find yourself scurrying around in your head trying to remember where you were supposed to focus your mindfulness, or if you find yourself controlling your breath, you need to relax. You are trying too hard and in an unhelpful way.

True mindfulness is an awareness that develops when our mind stays in contact with whatever we are doing. Mindfulness always has an object: It is always mindfulness of something. When we focus on our breathing, our mindfulness develops as our mind stays in contact with our breathing. It is really that simple. We do not have to do anything special or fancy. All of the different practice aids — gathas, guided meditations, mantras — are just ways to encourage us to keep our minds in contact with what is happening in the present moment. At some point, these aids drop away, and we are there, exposing ourselves to the moment as directly and with as much sincerity as we can.

Offering ourselves sincerely to the moment is the key to good practice. Our intention in practicing mindfulness is more important than any technique. Many meditation teachers have pointed out that all the skill and effort in meditation will not yield fruit if we do not have this sincere desire to wake up. In Buddhism this desire is called *bodhicitta,* which means the energy of awakening. Bodhicitta embodies our deepest desire to be loving, peaceful, and joyful, and to offer these qualities to others. Five minutes of practice with the sincere desire to wake up to the present moment is worth more than a lifetime of practice without it.

Of course, the Buddha did offer many different techniques for developing mindfulness and understanding human nature. But these are no more than a finger pointing at the moon. If we confuse the finger with the moon, if we think about it instead of doing it, or if we think that self-conscious practice of any technique is mindfulness, we do so at our peril. As we move into the practice of guided meditations that help us establish mindfulness, it can help us to remember this often.

As we do the practices of mindfulness more deeply, we "dis-identify" from things. Dis-identification in mindfulness practice is easily misunderstood; it's a term that might benefit from further explanation.

Dis-identification in mindfulness practice is a way of being more expansive and inclusive, not less. As we practice establishing mindfulness in our body, our feelings, our thinking, and our objects of mind, we come to realize that we are more than the body or the feeling or the thinking process or the object of our thinking. My own experience of this is a spaciousness that develops within the body, within the feeling, around the thinking or the object of thinking, almost as though a space existed between the inside of my skull and my mind. This does not mean that I dissociate myself from my body, feeling, thinking, or thought. I embrace it completely. As I embrace it, the spaciousness automatically opens.

Don't put any special effort into making this happen. When we try to make it happen, we create the expectation of a certain experience, which becomes yet another barrier. Remember, one of our jobs in mindfulness practice is to clear away expectations and preconceptions so that we can see things as they truly are. Expectation can be the obstacle that prevents us from being truly present.

In mindfulness practice, dis-identification means that we do not hold ourselves apart from or superior to anything, including our bodies, our feelings, our thinking, and the objects of our mind. Our practice thereby stays completely engaged. We do not attempt to establish anything outside of or within ourselves — a witness or an observer — that is separate from our present experience. Instead, we practice with a "witness consciousness" that is inextricably linked to, and intimately a part of, what we experience right now. We enter into the experience, and we allow the experience and ourselves to open.

In each of the guided meditations, conscious breathing is the anchor for our exploration. We do our best to be aware of our breathing at the same time that we are aware of the body or of the feelings, thinking, or objects of mind that arise and pass away. This is like patting the top of our heads and rubbing our bellies at the same time: It is daunting at first, but with practice it becomes easier. Before each instruction in the gatha, you will find the word *In* or *Out* in parentheses. This is a reminder to be aware of your in-breath and out-breath. It does not mean that you can only practice the instruction in the line that begins with "In" on the in-breath, or vice versa. While you are practicing with the guidance provided by that particular gatha, please practice it as a whole, not as two pieces broken apart by your in-breath and out-breath. I have had some students do that, and I've even tried it myself, and it is very confusing and artificial. Please avoid it.

In most of the sections that follow, you will find two sets of guided meditations (except in this section, which contains only one). The first meditation of each set is designed to build on the previous section's practice. The second meditation expands the practice in a new direction. Please be sure to do the first guided meditation in each section for one week. It will increase your ability to remain present and engaged with the thoughts, feelings, and sensations that naturally arise in sitting meditation. You may want to save the second meditation in the set for a later time, especially if you find it difficult to maintain stable concentration in your sitting practice. You can always come back to the second meditation in any of these sets when you are ready.

GUIDED MEDITATION ON
MINDFULNESS OF THE BODY

1. *(In) I know I am breathing in.*   IN
   (Out) I know I am breathing out.   OUT

2. *(In) I am aware of the hair*
   on top of my head.   HAIR ON HEAD
   (Out) I smile to the hair on my head. SMILING

Proceed in the same way through the body heading down toward the feet.

3. *(In) I am aware of the soles*
   of my feet.   SOLES OF FEET
   (Out) I smile to the soles of my feet. SMILING

4. *(In) I dwell in the present moment.*   PRESENT MOMENT
   (Out) I am aware this is the
   only moment
   when I am alive.   ONLY MOMENT

The first establishment of mindfulness is in the body. This is designed to help us experience "the body in the body," that is, truly to be the body as it experiences itself. In this meditation, we bring ourselves to different areas of our body. We become aware of that area of the body and then smile to it. The smile establishes an attitude of loving-kindness and compassion.

We usually start with the hair on top of our heads and go down our bodies to our feet. It helps to spend as much time as we need at each point in our body to allow some spaciousness to open up there. If you find areas that are tight, painful, or constricted you may want to spend more time there. Don't be surprised if you find thoughts or feelings arising as you spend time focusing your awareness on that painful part of your body. Tightness or pain gives tangible form to some emotional or spiritual discomfort; mindfulness of that body part will help you to see what it is. Please also remember that you don't have to do anything about the pain. Just by focusing your mindful concentration on the pain, it will reveal its true nature to you and will change, all without any striving on your part.

Many meditations like this are offered today. How is this meditation different, for example, from a body scan? In a body scan, you might just scan your body for problem areas. In a more therapeutic type of body meditation, you might use your breath to promote the release of tensions or thoughts and feelings that are held in different areas of your body. These meditations are all helpful, but their intention is not to establish mindfulness of the body in the body.

In this meditation, we enter deeply into the awareness of our body just for the sake of awakening to our body as a physical form. Only the breath and the body exist in this meditation: the body experiencing itself as a body through the sincere desire to be awake to the present moment. If release happens, that's fine; if it doesn't happen, that's fine also. What is important is to refrain from trying to make release, or anything else in particular, happen. All you need to do is focus your concentration on each part of your body, and let your breathing and your concentration do the rest. The real point is to be completely present in this moment. Meditation on the "body in the body" is simply one way to do that.

The more deeply we enter into our body or any part of it, the more likely it is to reveal its true nature to us. Understanding the true nature of things is an important part of mindfulness meditation. This is not a self-conscious study. Our analytical mind will not help us here. Our object is not to tick off the attributes of each of our body parts. Instead, we want to encourage ourselves to be still, to be aware of that part of the body, and even if just for a split second, to become aware of how we experience that part of the body, without putting labels on it. We may know that our bodies are made up of water and various minerals, but if we find our conscious minds reeling off a laundry list of what's in our livers we are probably going about the meditation in the wrong way. If we focus our attention on our livers and become aware of what comes up naturally, we might find our livers are composed of stars, sunshine, the fat from the cheese on the pizza we ate last night, or our anger at our noisy neighbor. It's all there, just as water is, or iron and bile, but it's hidden from us unless we enter deeply and without preconceptions into contemplation of our livers.

We maintain, in mindfulness meditation, a balance of unself-conscious awareness and attentive concentration. We are at once still and actively engaged. We may experience our stillness as the breath breathing itself (breathing without a breather) or as the heart experiencing itself as a heart (heart beating without a beater). At the moment when your stillness allows you to drop into this deep, concentrated awareness, you are actively engaged in your breath and your body, and the barrier between observer and object dissolves. You are like the scientist who suddenly realizes that she cannot be a separate observer, that by the mere process of observation she becomes part of the events that unfold. You are no longer trying to make anything happen; you are just being there, completely present and open and actively engaged in the present moment. That is the definition of being awake.

Please remember that when you smile to a part of your body, you are simply setting a direction. Most of us have complex and frequently unhealthy relationships with different parts of our bodies. If we have difficulties with our thighs, for example, we may find it hard to feel compassion or loving-kindness toward them. My ears hear moderately well, my feet support me with arch supports, my hands do what I need them to do, and my eyes see well with eyeglasses. I smile easily to all these parts of my body. When I was diagnosed with cancer in my mouth, however, I found it a lot harder for me to smile to my upper gums, where the cancer was located. In the weeks prior to surgery, I spent much time in sitting meditation getting acquainted with the cancer in my mouth and going through my feelings of fear and disappointment. I smiled all right, but the smile set a direction for practice for me, a direction of acceptance and compassion.

So please continue to smile if you can, and please remember that the smile is simply your North Star, pointing toward compassion. At the same time, please be aware of the feelings that come up: your fear, your displeasure, your anguish, your shame. In our guided meditation next week, we will develop ways of exploring the feelings contained in our bodies in more detail. This week, simply be aware of the feelings, and return to your mindful breathing and your awareness of your body.

This guided meditation is well suited to the body awareness that we have been exploring over the past two weeks. In fact, they are two different aspects of the same practice — establishing mindfulness in the body — and each one supports and feeds the other.

You can do a shortened version of this guided meditation when you first sit down to practice. In the shortened version, you may spend ten to twenty in- and out-breaths on each part of your body, and select one or two parts of your head, torso, and extremities. This short version can help you orient yourself to the present moment by bringing you into your body. When you do the full version of this guided meditation, you will want to spend at least five minutes on each part of your body, and you may spread the meditation out over several sitting periods. When you do the meditation this deeply, it can also be a doorway to enlightenment and liberation. I hope you find it enjoyable and rewarding.

HOME PLAY

FORMAL PRACTICE: Try doing the gatha-guided meditation on mindfulness of the body every other day. It helps to finish each session of this guided meditation with about five minutes of kinhin walking to help establish mindfulness of the body in motion and to include body awareness of sitting and standing. On the alternate days, begin your sitting meditation by counting the breath, and then by dropping away any reminders except for awareness of breathing and the question "What is this?" Continue your practice of developing an awareness of the spaciousness within your breath. Invite the sounds in your environment into the space within your breath. Hold the question "What is this?" about everything you encounter in your sitting and walking meditation. On the alternate days, see how the practices of guided and open sitting meditation work with each other.

INFORMAL PRACTICE: Try making the first five or ten minutes of each meal an occasion for silent, mindful eating. Do "telephone meditation": Every time the telephone rings, stop whatever you are doing and breathe in and out. Let the phone ring three times and then answer it. This runs counter to how most of us relate to the ringing tele-phone; usually, we jump to answer it! Do one daily-life mindfulness activity with the question "What is this?" Try doing your body awareness activities with an increased focus on at least one part of your body for each movement or posture.

GUIDED MEDITATIONS OF FEELINGS

FIRST MEDITATION

(In) I know I am breathing in.	IN
(Out) I know I am breathing out.	OUT
(In) I am aware of my whole body.	AWARE OF BODY
(Out) I smile to my body.	SMILING
(In) I am aware of a place in my body where I have pain or discomfort.	AWARE OF PAIN OR DISCOMFORT
(Out) I welcome the pain or discomfort and smile to it with compassion.	WELCOMING AND SMILING
(In) I am aware of the pain or discomfort as it changes.	DISCOMFORT CHANGING
(Out) I am aware of the pain or discomfort getting stronger or weaker.	DISCOMFORT STRONGER OR WEAKER
(In) I am aware of the feeling that lies at the heart of this pain or discomfort.	FEELING AT THE HEART
(Out) I am aware of the nature of this feeling.	NATURE OF THE FEELING
(In) I dwell in the present moment.	PRESENT MOMENT
(Out) I am aware this is the only moment when I am alive.	ONLY MOMENT

SECOND MEDITATION

(In) I know I am breathing in.	IN
(Out) I know I am breathing out.	OUT
(In) I am aware of a pleasant feeling arising in me.	PLEASANT FEELING
(Out) I am aware that I like having this feeling.	AWARE OF LIKING IT
(In) I hold this feeling as though it were my most precious child.	HOLDING THE FEELING
(Out) I smile with joy at my happiness.	SMILING WITH JOY
(In) I am aware of an unpleasant feeling arising in me.	UNPLEASANT FEELING
(Out) I am aware that I dislike having this feeling.	AWARE OF DISLIKING IT
(In) I hold this feeling as though it were my most precious child.	HOLDING THE FEELING
(Out) I smile with compassion at my suffering.	SMILING WITH COMPASSION
(In) I am aware of the feeling arising in me right now.	AWARE OF MY FEELING ARISING
(Out) I am aware of that feeling changing and passing away.	AWARE OF MY FEELING PASSING
(In) I dwell in the present moment.	PRESENT MOMENT
(Out) I am aware this is the only moment when I am alive.	ONLY MOMENT

MINDFULNESS
IN FEELINGS

In Buddhist psychology, consciousness is divided into two realms. One is called "storehouse consciousness." In the storehouse are all the seeds of every thought, feeling, or awareness we, or anyone else, could ever have. In Western psychological terms, the storehouse could be called a combination of the subconscious, unconscious, and collective unconscious. The other consciousness is called "mind consciousness." This is the area where we focus our conscious awareness. In Western psychological terms, this could be called the conscious mind. At various times, seeds from the storehouse consciousness come up into the mind consciousness. These feelings and thoughts are in our conscious mind from moment to moment. Most of the time, these seeds come into our mind consciousness uninvited; that is, they appear there because we encounter something that stimulates those seeds. If we look at a flower, a seed of happiness might be stimulated; if we have hay fever and look at a flower, a seed of annoyance might be stimulated along with a seed of sneeze anticipation. When a seed rises frequently from the storehouse consciousness into the mind consciousness, it grows stronger. For example, the seed of our anger grows ever more powerful when we constantly stimulate it.

Some seeds in us are so strong that when they are stimulated and rise into our mind consciousness, they overwhelm us and seem to leave no space for anything else. These, our most deeply ingrained, chronic issues, are the seeds that run us. When they overwhelm the mind consciousness, we are truly out of control; the seeds of our chronic pattern are in charge.

Feeling-states, such as pain, joy, anger, sadness, hope, and grief, all exist as seeds in our storehouse consciousness. Each of these feelings arises, sometimes subtly and sometimes in great washes, when we encounter something in our lives that stimulates that seed. When I was in high school, one young man who became a close friend of mine was German. As a young Jew, in the years after World War II and the Holocaust, I had to encounter the seeds of hatred and fear that this young man stimulated in me before he and I could become friends. I did not ask those seeds to come up; they arose naturally because of who each of us happened to be. Nearly every situation in life evokes some feeling-state, and this process that I experienced in getting to know my friend in high school occurs all the time. We are simply more or, mostly, less aware of it.

The Buddha identified feelings as one of the four areas where it is helpful to establish habits of mindfulness. So far, in sitting or walking meditation, we have allowed ourselves to be one with the feelings that rise and fall from moment to moment. In Zen, we refer to this process as allowing the thought-feeling mass to melt slowly in the light of our conscious awareness. This is the first approach to mindfulness of feelings: being aware of what we are feeling when we are feeling it.

We expand on this approach in the first guided meditation in this section. Taking up where our meditation on mindfulness of the body leaves off, we begin by focusing on areas of our bodies where we feel pain or discomfort and enter more deeply and directly into those feelings. Usually, pain or discomfort is a manifestation of tightness or tension in our bodies, which in turn is a manifestation of other, more deeply seated emotions. When we breathe mindfully with awareness of the parts of our bodies, our tension and pain have a chance to dissipate. Doing mindful breathing in this way is like a massage: It brings blood to that area of our bodies and helps them to heal.

We go deeper, allowing our mindfulness to touch the nature of the feeling that lies at the heart of that part of our bodies. Now we have touched several seeds in the storehouse consciousness: the seed of mindfulness, the seed of pain, and the seed of the feelings that lie within the muscles or joints in our bodies that have been in pain. By doing this, we allow ourselves to encounter the feeling and to notice how it is contained in the body even though it is made of a different substance.

As we do this guided meditation, we hold ourselves steady with each feeling as it arises. Our purpose here is to engage actively in the feeling without being overwhelmed by it. We accept the feeling, welcome it, and acknowledge that it is part of us. We remember to stay grounded in our bodies, to experience the feeling without spinning off into thought. This is the process of being present with the feeling.

Most of us find it difficult to be present with our feelings. When a feeling is one we label "good," like joy or pleasure, we want to grab onto it and fix it permanently in time and space. When the feeling is one we label "bad," we want to avoid it. As ways to avoid the reality of what we are feeling, we usually engage either in dramatizing the feeling — acting it out — or in suppressing it. Neither approach really allows us to stay steady with our feelings. When we act our feelings out, we may think we're getting rid of them, when all we're doing is making the seeds of those feelings stronger by feeding them. When we deny or suppress our feelings, we may think they will not bother us. In fact we're creating a big pressure cooker. Sooner or later the feelings we didn't want to know about will explode and we will end up acting them out anyway. When a friend asks you if you are having a nice day and gets a tirade of everything that's gone wrong for the last ten years, you can be sure you've suppressed some strong anger, hurt, or resentment, and that you are acting it out on your friend. Even if you don't act the feeling out, the drama you create around the feeling — the story you tell yourself about what caused it, why you feel the way you do, who is responsible, and so on — creates far more suffering for you than the feeling itself does. In Shakespeare's play by the same name, Othello creates a terrible drama out of his inability to tolerate his feelings of jealousy; ultimately, he destroys himself and his beloved

Desdemona. We create dramas of our own all the time; drama is a habit of avoidance just as potent as suppression.

As we engage in the process of being mindful of feelings, we soon realize that neither suppression nor drama really work. Instead, if we can allow ourselves to stay steady with our feelings in the first guided meditation, if we let our thought-feeling mass melt slowly in the light of our conscious awareness, we discover the great power in simply being present with our feelings. When we abandon suppression and disengage from drama, we suddenly find ourselves present with what we have most feared: our feelings. Then something happens. We may notice that a spaciousness opens in the mind consciousness, almost as though our very beings have expanded. Simply having room in the mind consciousness for mindfulness of breathing while at the same time we are feeling shame or despair allows us to be present with the reality that we are, in fact, more than our shame or despair. If conscious breathing is in your mind consciousness, then you can be aware that you are your conscious breathing, too. I use shame and despair here as examples (they are two of my major chronic feeling states), and I encourage you to substitute your own.

Your shame or despair is one form of energy; your mindfulness is another form of energy. The process of developing true understanding of your feelings happens when the energy of mindfulness embraces the energy of your shame or despair. Imagine that you hold your shame in your arms as gently as though it were your baby. If you can take this approach, you will find that your relationship with your shame changes: You are no longer its victim, no longer the subject of the drama. You may even notice that you are aware of the sound of a car passing by or the warmth of the sunshine. You don't hide in these; you simply allow them to coexist with your shame. With this balance, you can stay steady enough with your shame so that it can reveal its true nature to you.

But what does this mean, "reveal its true nature"? When we truly disengage from the drama and the narrative we create around the feeling, when we enter into an awareness of the feeling without judgment, without opinions, and without labels, we encounter the feeling itself. And that may be very different from what we imagine the feeling is. Zen Master Bo Mun likes to say, "Don't give back to the pain any more than it gives to you." If you have a pain in your leg, you may be more aware of your feelings about the pain — your fear of pain, your anger at being hurt, your desire to be free of pain — than you are of the pain itself. The pain is simply pain; what we give back to it is our opinion of the pain (we don't like it), our judgment of the pain (it's bad), and our label for it (the word and concept of "pain," with all the emotional freight that goes with it). When we are present with the pain in this way, without concepts, opinions, and judgments, we are present with it in true mindfulness. And free from our opinions and judgments, the pain can simply be there and show us its true face.

The second guided meditation continues the exploration begun in the first. Here we allow ourselves to focus more directly on that "like/don't like" attitude we have toward our thoughts and feelings. The Buddha called this "attachment" and "aversion," and he saw clearly how essential the attitude is to how we create suffering for ourselves. He reminded us that this attachment/aversion polarity is the source of all of our suffering, which is just another way of saying that it's our attitude toward what we encounter in life that creates suffering. Attachment and aversion put us at war with life because the basic reality of life is that things change: What we want and what we don't want come to us and then go away. We don't like this and we try to control it, but no matter how hard we try, the reality of change, or impermanence, remains.

When we want to free ourselves from suffering, we work in meditation (sitting, walking, eating, daily mindfulness) to free ourselves enough from attachment and aversion so that whatever happens in our lives, no matter how beautiful or difficult, is okay. This does not mean we become emotional zombies who only have neutral feelings. It also doesn't mean we become passive victims of circumstance. It means allowing ourselves to feel joy, sadness, excitement, and anger, and at the same time not to prefer one feeling to the other. In this way, we don't hang on to the feelings we like (and suffer when those feelings pass away, which they inevitably do), and we don't push away the feelings we don't like (and suffer when the feelings we suppressed come roaring back to haunt us later).

As we work with these guided meditations over time, and as the spaciousness opens further inside the mind consciousness, we can become aware of that same spaciousness opening within a feeling when we focus our true mindful awareness on it. In this space within the feeling, there are no words or labels, no concepts. Free of concepts, we can touch the feeling directly, even if only for a fraction of a moment. When we do, when we allow whatever it is to just be there in true mindfulness, compassion naturally arises. This is the awareness of the feeling within the feeling, the awareness of the true nature of the feeling from inside itself, where there is no separation between us and the feeling. We may even sense that the feeling we have is not ours alone. For example, we may become aware of vast, endless anger instead of our own separate anger. We may find arising unbidden in ourselves an awareness of the anger of a Bosnian Serb toward a Bosnian Muslim or of the grief and joy of a prisoner being released and reunited with his family. This may sound overwhelming, but when it happens, there is no sense of being overwhelmed by anger, grief, or joy. Instead, there is only a sense of the endless love and compassion of the universe in its unlimited manifestations, and the strong loving-kindness and compassion for everyone because we all have these feelings.

This is not an abstract exercise; it has very concrete results.

In early 2000, I underwent surgery to remove cancer from my mouth. This entailed removing several teeth, the upper jawbone they were attached to, the surrounding gum tissue, and a portion of my hard palate. Going into the surgery, I requested the lightest anesthetic possible and no narcotic painkillers. I awoke from the surgery with a throbbing feeling in my head and otherwise relatively clearheaded and alert. I managed my pain with a combination of mindful breathing and regular Tylenol. The "true face" of pain was simply, moment to moment, what I was feeling, and that was okay, that was manageable.

Nothing I did here was out of the range of any person who practices mindfulness. I could only do this because I had practiced a lot with my feelings for the six weeks prior to the surgery. Jon Kabat-Zinn likes to say that practicing mindfulness is like knitting a parachute; if we work on it diligently, it's there when we need it. That was true for me. As a result of practice, I didn't get hung up in the drama of the cancer surgery ("How has this happened to me?" "I'm going to die," "What did I do to deserve this?" "My life is ruined," and so on) or resist the reality of my pain. I had feelings, for sure, but it was all okay. The pain was okay and my life was still okay, even though it was far different than it had been two months earlier, when there was no evidence of cancer. My practice had led me to an understanding that living with pain, or even awareness of my mortality, was (and is) my reality. I did my best not to suppress or to dramatize; instead, I tried to be simply, moment to moment, with what is. From that space, I had equanimity and compassion for myself and for everyone around me, and everyone around me — my wife, friends, doctors, and nurses — benefited from this.

Balance is extremely important in these meditations. We must understand the limits of what we can handle at any given moment. If our mindfulness is strong, we can handle a lot of suffering. If our mindfulness is not so strong, suffering will overwhelm us. Some people say they felt as though they were going to drown in their feelings when describing this state. When you find yourself getting overwhelmed like this, and your mindfulness is not strong enough to keep you stable, stop the meditation and do some walking meditation, preferably outdoors, or something else that you really enjoy. This will help you bring your attention more toward the world around you, and that will balance things out. Before you try the meditation on that feeling again, give yourself some time to establish mindfulness of your breathing. Doing a mindfulness of body meditation may also be helpful.

Meditation on feelings is strong medicine. The practice of waking up to our "like/don't like" mind and our acceptance of what is going on right now awaken within us loving-kindness and compassion. It is the root of the Buddhist meditation on loving-kindness called *metta* or *maitri* and of the meditation on compassion called *karuna*. It is worth a lifetime of practice.

MINDFUL EXERCISE

Most of us engage in some form of exercise. We may walk, jog, run, hike, swim, ski, kayak, snowboard, surf; or perhaps we use exercise machines, such as treadmills, or rowing machines, or weight training machines. This exercise is good for us. It helps us to maintain healthy bodies and helps our minds by increasing the blood flow to the brain.

We do some kinds of exercise on autopilot. We frequently jog wearing headphones. We walk on treadmills while we read the newspaper or a book. We use ski machines and watch television at the same time. Would you call this mindful exercise? Our bodies are exercising, but where are our minds? Our bodies are working and our minds are off listening to music or watching the news. We certainly are not engaged with what our bodies are doing.

Most of us use the headphones, books, newspapers, or television to avoid boredom. This is especially true when we use exercise machines. After all, we tell ourselves, we are making the same, repetitive stationary motions. How could that be anything but boring?

Mindful exercise, as you might guess, means keeping body and mind involved together in the exercise activity. We can jog outdoors without headphones just as we do walking meditation. We can be aware of our jogging legs, our pumping arms, our heart and lungs working together, and we can also notice the blue sky and the sound of the birds. Why must we blast music into our brains when these miracles are present to us? Our headphones, books, and televisions dissociate us from our exercising bodies and from the world around us.

When we exercise mindfully, we maintain our awareness of what our bodies are doing. We stay aware of our breathing, of our legs and arms moving rhythmically, and we have the opportunity to become even more aware of our hearts and lungs working together. We can stay in contact with our breathing, we can notice how it becomes deeper and more rapid, we can feel the connection between our moving arms and legs and our in-breath and out-breath. From a very practical point of view, mindful exercise makes it far less likely that we will injure ourselves. If we are truly paying attention to our breathing and our exercising body, we will be aware the moment a muscle starts to feel even slightly overstressed.

Try to use your old friend, the question "What is this?" about the different parts of your moving body as you exercise. Keep the open mind of "I don't know," and with that openness move more deeply into your body and your movement. As you expand your awareness into your exercise, as you experience ever more easily the motionless center inside your movement, you can allow a timeless space to open, where there is just breathing, just moving, and no breather, no mover. We can change the old Zen exhortation to "In the jogging, only the jogging. In the breathing, only the breathing."

HOME PLAY

FORMAL PRACTICE: Try doing the first guided meditation on feeling every other day. On the alternate days, you can continue your practice of counting the breath and entering into awareness of thoughts and feelings — using "What is this"/"I don't know" — or if you enjoy the guided meditation on the body, you can continue with that. Try ending each period of sitting meditation with a few minutes of kinhin walking meditation.

INFORMAL PRACTICE: Add another daily-life mindfulness activity from the list that has a gatha for it, and use the gatha while you do this activity as a way of helping you to focus your attention. Try doing mindful exercise at least once during the week. Continue your mindful meals. Make every time you walk an occasion for walking meditation.

Guided Meditations of Thinking

FIRST MEDITATION

(In) I know I am breathing in.   IN
(Out) I know I am breathing out.   OUT

(In) I am aware of the beginning of a thought
    as it arises in my mind.   THOUGHT ARISING
(Out) I smile to this arising thought.   SMILING

(In) I am aware of the end of a thought as it
    passes away from my mind.   THOUGHT PASSING
(Out) I smile to this passing thought.   SMILING

(In) I am aware of the point when one thought
    passes away and another thought arises.   THOUGHTS ENDING AND BEGINNING
(Out) I am aware of the space between the
    thoughts in my mind.   SPACE BETWEEN THOUGHTS

(In) I am aware that I am not caught
    up in my thinking.   NOT CAUGHT
(Out) I feel calm and stable.   CALM AND STABLE

(In) I dwell in the present moment.   PRESENT MOMENT
(Out) I know this is the only moment
    when I am alive.   ONLY MOMENT

SECOND MEDITATION

(In) I know I am breathing in.   IN
(Out) I know I am breathing out.   OUT

(In) I am aware of thoughts arising.   THOUGHTS ARISE
(Out) I am aware of thoughts passing away.   THOUGHTS PASSING

(In) I am aware of my judgments of my
    thinking and breathing arising.   JUDGMENT THOUGHTS ARISE
(Out) I realize the suffering my judgments
    cause me, and smile with compassion.   SMILING

(In) I am aware of my judgments of my
    thinking and breathing passing away.   JUDGMENT THOUGHTS PASS
(Out) I release all of the suffering my
    judgments create in my body and mind.   RELEASE

(In) I dwell in the present moment.   PRESENT MOMENT
(Out) I am aware this is the only moment
    when I am alive.   ONLY MOMENT

MINDFULNESS
IN THINKING

W hen most of us are introduced to the practice of meditation and mindfulness, usually our opinion is that thinking is bad. After all, we reason, our thinking and ideas have become a layer between the present moment and ourselves. Our mind has convinced us that we are isolated. At least, that is how we often perceive the situation.

Of course, our mind's job is to think. Just as our stomach's job is to digest food, and our eye's job is to see, our mind's job is to generate thought. Remember how Larry Rosenberg, in his admonition in the "Third Week" section, says "when" our mind wanders, not "if"? We cannot stop the thinking process, any more than we can stop the sound of the river. What we can do is liberate ourselves from the tyranny of an undisciplined and rampaging mind. We can do this by understanding the mind better.

The Buddha reminded us that the door to our liberation from suffering lies in seeing clearly how our minds work. In fact, thinking is neither good nor bad; it simply exists, it's neutral. Our relationship to our thinking can be productive or unproductive, positive or negative. So thinking can (and will) go on; that's fine. To encourage a positive relationship with thinking, we put our attention on the nature of thinking itself and the kinds of thoughts we generate. In this way, we get to know how our thinking minds work. As we get clearer and clearer about the nature of thinking, we are less attached to each thought, less inclined to follow it out to its conclusion or to believe that this one thought is the only reality that exists. In this way, our relationship to our thinking changes, and our liberation begins.

The gathas across from the opening of this chapter present two basic guided meditations on the nature of thinking. In the first, we focus on the process of thinking itself, with particular attention to where one thought ends and another begins, and to the fact that a space (however minute) is between them.

It takes some awareness to notice that our thoughts naturally arise and pass away, even the ones that seem the most stubborn. At times our minds will enter what seems to be an endless stream of repetitive or circuitous thinking. We feel helpless to interrupt the cycle, and we feel that the cycle of thoughts will always be there. In some people this problem goes to its extreme and produces what we call obsessive thinking. At the other extreme, we can get so scattered in our thinking that we can't keep our minds concentrated on anything for more than a few moments. The mind becomes a wild beast, which it seems we can never bring under control.

One of the greatest values of mindfulness meditation is how it can help us to see the true nature of thinking:

Thoughts are not permanent; they arise and they fall away. Most of us experience following a train of thought, only to find ourselves on a byway that somehow leads us back to the original thought, which then changes and goes on to a totally unrelated thought, and then to . . . the list goes on. Even if the thoughts rise and fall, the process of thinking seems so persistent and uncontrollable that the thoughts take us careening off into — where? Someplace other than here, for sure. If you find this kind of thinking going on, you aren't alone. All of us do this.

If we want to free ourselves from the tyranny of the thinking mind, we need to change our relationships to our thinking and our thoughts. To do this, we will focus first on the process of thinking itself.

In this first meditation, we focus on our awareness of our thinking rather than on the thoughts themselves. We can do this more easily if we have established a strong sitting meditation practice. One benefit of sitting meditation is that as we sit more and for longer sessions, our thinking becomes slower. Our thoughts are like waves on the ocean: When we do sitting meditation, the ocean grows calmer and the waves come less frequently. As our thought processes slow down, we can become more intimately aware of them. As we are more intimately aware of them, we understand better the true nature of our minds. When we concentrate on thinking rather than on each individual thought, we tend not to follow each thought down its byway. This is called "following the mindfulness road," rather than "following the mind road." The mind road gets caught up in the thinking. The mindfulness road is aware of the thinking but doesn't "follow" it. To do this, we must maintain an awareness of our breathing. Conscious breathing becomes an anchor. With the anchor of following the in and out nature of our breath, we can allow thinking to be present without getting caught up in it.

This step — awareness of breathing and of thinking — is one of the first and most important you will take to develop your awareness of the true nature of your thinking. To do this meditation well, you must keep both breathing and thinking alive in your awareness at the same time. This is the beginning of establishing what we call "witness consciousness." The witness, commonsensically, observes what is going on. I experience the witness as the spaciousness of the breath, that "shaving the inside of the skull" awareness we discussed during the fifth week. The witness allows us to be present to our thinking and our feelings, with an awareness that something else is there besides the thinking or the feelings. That "something," the witness, is the part of ourselves where compassion and loving-kindness live.

You need to realize that this witness is not a separate entity, and it does not stand apart from what it is witnessing. It is only one aspect of consciousness, and it is not separate from the other aspects of consciousness. There is danger in creating a separate, self-conscious witness: When we do that, we stand apart from what is being witnessed, and we then begin to stand apart from life and to divorce ourselves from reality. We convince ourselves that we are only the witness, and that the thoughts we are witnessing are separate from us. Instead, if you enter deeply into the body of your thinking by holding your thinking and your breathing in the light of your mindfulness and concentration, you are establishing a direct, clear connection between your witness (mindfulness) and the object you are witnessing (thinking).

How do you do this? Breathe and hold steady. Keep your attention focused on your breathing and your thinking. As your thoughts move, your thinking will move and your mind will stay still. If this sounds confusing, try the guided meditation for a while and notice your experience. The core essence of this meditation is stillness and stability, an unmoving steadiness where the waves of thought and the mind ride each other and become one. Your witness and the object of your witnessing will show themselves as different and the same, separate and entwined.

To reach this steadiness, focus on the points where each thought begins and where it ends. By doing this, you will see your thinking without focusing unduly on each individual thought. This emphasis will help you to avoid the mind road and stay on the mindfulness road.

The first meditation is structured to help you be aware of the different stages of the thinking process: first the point where a thought arises, then the point where the thought passes away, and finally the point where one thought ends and another begins. In my classes, this is probably the most challenging meditation for most people. You can make it simpler for yourself by not getting too hung up on the instructions. See if you can become aware of when a thought arises; perhaps when you do this, you become even more aware that another thought has ended. That's fine. The purpose of this meditation is to experience the wavelike motion of thinking — the rising and falling — and to experience riding the wave of thought. When we ride the wave of thinking, we are still, even though thinking is going on. We identify less with our thinking; we realize that it is only part of us, simply a function of the mind, and not our essence. This is a twist on Descartes's famous "I think, therefore I am." We might say, "I am, and my mind thinks." You may experience this for only a moment; that's fine. In my experience, focusing on the space between the thoughts is the most helpful way to do this. The more you do this meditation, the more established you become in riding the wave of thinking. Please be patient with yourself.

There is a story about a Zen student who kept pestering his teacher to tell him the secret of awakening. After being asked so many times, the teacher finally got annoyed. He said to his student, "You know the space between your thoughts?" The student eagerly answered, "Yes, yes!!" The teacher said, "Well, make it larger!" We don't want to artificially force anything, so "making" the space larger is not a good idea. But you will find that the space between the thoughts will naturally grow larger the more you practice this meditation. The waves calm down, and the space between them grows.

In the second meditation we deliberately focus on one particular thought pattern, that of judgment thoughts. I expect that everyone who has ever meditated has experienced judgment thoughts: "I'm not breathing properly," "I'll never reach enlightenment with this posture," "I can't stop thinking," "I've failed because I can't follow my breath 100 percent of the time."... Do you recognize yourself somewhere in that list? We then judge ourselves for being judgmental; after all, we're not supposed to judge ourselves. With each layer of judgment, we put another barrier between ourselves and being truly present in this moment. How can we be aware of the birdsong, the sound of the passing car, the silvery trees dressed in icicles, when all we are aware of is judgment, judgment, judgment?!

So this meditation works at helping us free ourselves from the trap of following our thinking and also helps us see that judgment thoughts are just like any other: They too arise and they pass away. We take advantage of the fact that we judge ourselves for thinking and turn the judgment to good use. Because we are focused on where each thought begins and where it ends, we become more aware of the pattern of the judgment thinking than we are of any individual thought. We stay tuned to our breathing. As we stray from awareness of the breath, a judgment thought arises. We notice the judgment thought's arising and then its natural passing away. When we see this pattern, we can see the prisons we have created for ourselves with our thinking. This simple awareness is the first step in transformation.

To keep steady, you need to be in balance. If conscious breathing is your anchor, smiling is your balance point. When you smile a smile of compassion, you are encouraging your loving-kindness to wake up. You are encouraging yourself to be kind to yourself because you are a thinking being. Of course, the energy of judgment stands in the way. By directing your compassion and loving-kindness to yourself, you create a balance to your judgment thinking.

Stay steady and concentrated and your mindfulness of thinking will deepen. As you penetrate more deeply into the pattern of judgment thinking, you will begin to understand the kind of suffering it causes you. If you are conscientious in directing your compassion and loving-kindness toward yourself, your awareness of this suffering will feed and stimulate these positive states of mind. Ultimately, if your mindfulness is strong enough, the compassion and loving-kindness you generate can allow you to stand firm in the presence of these rising and falling judgment thoughts without being caught up in them. They can be just what they are — thoughts that arise and pass away and don't run your life or your perception of yourself.

You can get the same results if you substitute any thought pattern with which you have trouble for judgment thoughts. Just remember that the focus is on a *pattern* of the thoughts, the *process* of thinking.

Like all of the other guided meditations we do, eventually the guidance can fall away, and we are simply there, breathing in and out, and thinking is going on. The cycles of this meditation — thoughts rising and falling, touching our suffering deeply and allowing it to go free — will happen automatically and without forethought. At this point, we can truly enter into the body of our thinking. Your awareness of yourself as a thinker can fall away, and you can be completely unself-consciously aware of thinking as thinking. In Zen, this awareness is expressed in the saying, "In the thinking, only what is thought." When this happens, you may become aware more deeply of the true nature of your thought process.

As the Buddhist understands it, thinking has three parts. The first part is the simple awareness of something. This awareness has no observer ("In the thinking, only what is thought"). Almost as soon as this awareness occurs, the second part happens, which is an awareness of the awareness, in other words, a self-consciousness. The third part takes the awareness and puts it into the context of comparisons and contrasts in our memory bank.

These three parts can happen so quickly that we aren't usually aware that they are discrete, but each of us has probably had one experience in our lives of finding our mind suddenly quiet, and then hearing a voice that arises in our mind saying something like "My mind is quiet. Isn't that interesting?" That commenting voice is the "awareness of awareness," the self-conscious narrative that results from our mind's natural process. Even though we spend most of our lives unconscious of our thinking process, all of us have at some point experienced this silence and commentary. We have experienced how our thinking mind packages the world for us.

Many years ago I sat a meditation retreat with Zen Master Su Bong. He was a monk of very deep experience, with many years of sitting, walking, eating, and working practice inside him. At the end of the retreat, he shared with us that at one point his mind had become completely clear, only breathing was happening, and then a thought came up: "I wonder what would happen if I won the New Hampshire lottery?" He then thought: "This is crazy. I'm a monk, I don't have money, and I don't play the lottery." The thoughts then went away, and his mind cleared again. Then another thought arose: "If I won the lottery, I could buy a boat." This led to another thought: "I don't own anything as a monk, and I wouldn't want a boat anyway." His mind cleared again. Then another thought arose: "If I bought a boat, I could give it to my friend who likes boats." And so it went. Each of his spontaneous thoughts — "I wonder what would happen if I won the lottery," "If I won the lottery, I could buy a boat," and "If I bought a boat, I could give it to my friend who likes boats" — arose naturally out of the silence of simply being present. With each thought that arose, Su Bong's mind commented on it and placed it in the context of his experience and his memories — "I'm a monk, I don't have money," and "I don't own anything as a monk." Su Bong's mind was doing its job, and his mind manifested thoughts out of the spaciousness of that present moment. All three aspects of the thinking process were present: the moment of pure awareness, the awareness of awareness, and then the "packaging" of the awareness through memory and experience.

Most of the time we remain unconscious of the narrative package and unaware that our thinking is telling us how to interpret what we perceive. As we do more sitting meditation and as our thinking starts to slow down, we can begin to develop awareness of each part of the thought process and disengage from our thinking. The deeper this awareness goes, the more immediate and unobstructed our contact becomes with the present moment. And then mindfulness can occur.

What happens in that moment of direct observation, before we label it, before the thoughts, before the symbolic and conceptual words come forward — what happens in that moment is authentic mindfulness. The space between the thoughts, the moment of quiet, nonverbal awareness, is the moment of mindfulness. Even when we put our hand on a light switch and recite a gatha, if there is no moment in that experience where the words drop away and we have a glimpse of unobstructed, present awareness, free of labels and concepts, there is no true mindfulness.

When we experience thoughts and the thinking process itself as ephemeral, we touch upon a deeper truth: Everything is ephemeral. We can see this clearly with our thoughts. A thought rises up and it passes away. We can even see it with our thinking process. Our thinking gets quieter and then it becomes more active. But that rising and falling nature is not limited to thoughts and thinking. As your practice deepens, you will see that everything in the world is like this. Your house, your chair, the sun and trees, and even your favorite friend are all ephemeral. They all manifest in their particular forms for a while and then they "unmanifest." In the Buddhist world this is called "impermanence," and the Buddha saw this under-standing to be crucial in freeing people from suffering and despair. Even your own self, your carefully con-structed package of identities and labels, is a construction of thoughts that rise up and pass away. This aspect of being that each of us calls "myself" is as ephemeral as the cloud passing by. This may be hard to remember when your thinking goes out of control or when your feelings overwhelm you. Because you can experience the ephemeral nature of thinking through mindfulness practice, as you have done in this section, you can free yourself when the difficult times arrive. We will explore impermanence more thoroughly in the next section.

The practice of sitting helps us to cultivate mindfulness — in the words of the frustrated Zen teacher, to make the space between our thoughts larger. Meditation on the process of thinking, especially as we do it in the first guided meditation, gives us one way in. How we manifest the practice in our daily life is our way out. You do not have to become a monk or live apart from the world to do this. It is possible for all of us. If we want our lives and our world to be better, it is necessary.

Home Play

FORMAL PRACTICE: Do the first guided meditation on thinking every other day. On the alternate days, you can continue your practice of counting the breath and entering into awareness of thoughts and feelings using "What is this"/"I don't know." Some of my students find it helpful to do a quick version of the meditation on the body to start these open sitting periods. End each period of sitting meditation with a few minutes of kinhin walking meditation.

INFORMAL PRACTICE: Add another daily-life mindfulness activity from the list, and write a gatha for it.
Continue your mindful meals and walking meditation.
When you are in a car (whether you're driving or a pas-
senger), try doing "red light meditation": Every time you
come to a red light, consider it a bell of mindfulness and
do mindful breathing while the light is red. You may find
your attitude toward red lights changes dramatically after
doing this for a week!

GUIDED MEDITATIONS ON OBJECTS OF MIND

FIRST MEDITATION

(In) I know I am breathing in.
IN

(Out) I know I am breathing out.
OUT

(In) I ask if my thought/feeling/perception creates suffering.
SUFFERING

(Out) I ask if my thought/feeling/perception creates well-being.
WELL-BEING

(In) I explore the contents of my thought/feeling/perception.
EXPLORING

(Out) I allow the true nature of my thought/feeling/perception to reveal itself.
REVEALING TRUE NATURE

(In) I ask who created this thought/feeling/perception.
WHO CREATED THIS

(Out) I answer and smile.
SMILING

(In) I ask if this thought/feeling/perception is all I am.
IS THIS ALL I AM?

(Out) I answer and smile.
SMILING

(In) I dwell in the present moment.
PRESENT MOMENT

(Out) I know this is the only moment when I am alive.
ONLY MOMENT

SECOND MEDITATION

(In) I know I am breathing in.
IN

(Out) I know I am breathing out.
OUT

(In) I am aware of a judgment thought arising within me.
JUDGMENT THOUGHTS ARISING

(Out) I hold steady with that judgment thought.
HOLDING STEADY

(In) I look deeply into the judgment thought.
LOOKING DEEPLY

(Out) I see the judgment thought is made up of different elements.
SEEING THE ELEMENTS

(In) I allow the different elements of the judgment thought to be present within me.
ELEMENTS PRESENT IN ME

(Out) I smile with compassion at the suffering these elements have caused.
SMILE WITH COMPASSION

(In) I dwell in the present moment.
PRESENT MOMENT

(Out) I am aware this is the only moment when I am alive.
ONLY MOMENT

MINDFULNESS IN OBJECTS OF MIND

The teaching on the Four Establishments of Mindfulness is one of many "how-to" talks the Buddha gave during his lifetime. These sutras are probably the earliest meditation manuals we have. They are very practical, offering graduated sets of instructions on where and how to focus our attention. The Buddha was a practical man, and he did his best to remind his students that they were to take the instructions he gave as guides for the practice of meditation and for living, and not as doctrines. He emphasized that our direct experience of meditation and of life is most important.

The Buddha instructed us that the fourth area in which we can establish mindfulness is what he termed "objects of mind." This means anything that our mind focuses on. The Buddha categorized objects of mind and suggested certain ones as the most appropriate subjects for meditation. One way, suggested by the Buddha in the Four Establishments of Mindfulness, is to focus on things that nourish the positive aspects of our being. The Buddha suggested several meditations in this vein; you will find them set out in Thich Nhat Hanh's *Healing and Transformation* (see "Recommended Reading") and in other meditation texts.

In the broadest sense, an "object of mind" can be any thought, feeling, or object of perception, and we approach "object of mind" meditation here in that broad context. We can establish mindfulness of any object of mind by holding our attention on it steadily. If we do this with sufficient energy and commitment, and with the clear intention to be awake, the "object of mind" unfolds its true nature before us. From this comes understanding. And from understanding comes freedom.

When we do "object of mind" meditation, we are focusing on how completely our mind creates our reality. Our first guided meditation in this section provides one simple way to do this. It is based on an instruction that the Buddha gave to his nine-year-old son Rahula about how to practice: He suggested that for every thought and feeling that came up, Rahula should ask, "Does this create well-being or does it create suffering?"

Here's an example: Recently I went hiking to one of my favorite spots in northern New Hampshire by a trail I had never used before. As I hiked up the trail, I was aware of how beautiful everything was, and I felt completely connected with the trail, the sunshine, the mountain — everything. The time went blissfully, and when I arrived at my destination (a small pond in the mountains) I felt as though I had hiked for only a short while. I spent some time at the pond, figuring I needed only a short time to hike back. As I hiked down, I kept looking at my watch and wondering why it was taking me so long. I knew that the gate out of the woods closed at a certain time and I began to panic. The trail felt very long, the trail and time became my enemies, and I felt alone and isolated.

Now this was the same trail, and I was certainly hiking downhill faster than I had hiked uphill, and still the trail was so much longer coming down than it had been going up! Why was this? It was all a creation of my mind. What "objects of mind" was my mind manufacturing and focusing on? Going up, my object of mind was my enjoyment of the mountain. Going down, my object of mind was my anxiety about being locked into the forest overnight. My mind created a beautiful reality in one moment and a fearful one in the next.

My years of practice helped me here. I felt tension in my body and was aware of my mental chatter. In a natural and unforced way, I began working with the process of the first guided meditation for this week. I knew I was creating suffering, because at some level I realized that the trail was the same one I had walked up and enjoyed a few hours before. I allowed myself to become one with my fear that I would be stuck in the forest overnight without adequate warm clothing and that something terrible would happen to me. I knew that my mind had created this anxiety, and as that awareness opened up, the trail opened up and I saw once again the birches. The fear was still there, but it no longer consumed me. I heard the sound of the brook and watched three partridges fly across my path. I was once again connected with everything. I realized that I had my car, that there were a couple of houses inside the forest, and even if there weren't, I would still find a way to survive the night.

So, was this a beautiful trail or not a beautiful trail? All of it, beautiful or not beautiful, I made in my mind. Once I realized this, I was free.

What we focus on can lead us in a particular direction; in my case, fear led to panic. One thing we learn pretty quickly by doing this practice is that our perception, or mind focus, does not operate independently of what we are perceiving or what our mind is focusing on. The connection is direct and exclusive. So if we focus on "Coca-Cola," we may find ourselves developing a thirst for caffeine and sugar! If we focus on thoughts of revenge, hatred and thoughts of violence may consume us.

Working with difficult and unpleasant objects of mind is essential to your practice. Your awareness of difficult and unpleasant things can be a door to transformation. In my hiking experience, I only thought of my options to survive because I allowed myself to go completely into my fear and anxiety. In the gatha meditation in the fourth week, we entered deeply into "frazzle" and it transformed into "calm." When you allow yourself to enter completely into the experience of your difficult state of mind, when you examine it thoroughly, the mist will part and you can see your way more clearly. While the object of mind itself will remain in your consciousness, perhaps dormant, perhaps coming up again at another time, your relationship to it changes: It will no longer consume you or run you. This changing relationship is the substance of transformation.

You will probably take a while to transform your relationships with chronic, deep-seated difficult or destructive objects of mind, whether they are mental states, feelings, or perceptions. I have seen this take months, sometimes years. You may have to do this again and again as new situations arise in your life that prompt new manifestations of the chronic problem. The depth of your trauma, the skill of your practice, and the support of your mindfulness-practice group and teacher are all elements that will influence how quickly or slowly this process goes.

When you are doing sitting meditation, your mindfulness must be strong if you are to focus on an object of mind that can lead you into danger. Our goal in this practice is to become more intimate with the object of mind, not to be overwhelmed by it. When we are overwhelmed, we drown. In everyday life, when we find these thoughts and feelings arising, the discipline of mindfulness, which you are developing through your mindfulness practice, helps us remain solid as our minds focus on the difficult or destructive objects of mind. The story of my hike is a good example of how this can work.

When you do the first guided meditation, you are entering into an investigative process. While it requires your attention and energy, it does not require or benefit from our traditional analytical thinking. Our analytical thinking takes us down the old, familiar paths in our minds and most frequently ends in a rehash of familiar arguments and defenses. You want to allow yourself to relax into this process. This is the only way we can allow the content of the objects of mind — the ones we don't analytically understand and even the ones we don't want to know about — to reveal itself to us. It's how we allow new synapses to open in our brain and allow new pathways, unexpected ones, perhaps, to open in our mind.

From this new understanding you will forge a new, dynamic relationship with the object of mind.

The first guided meditation can be done either as an "open meditation," in which you allow yourself to become aware of whatever your mind focuses on as you sit; or it can be done as a "closed meditation," in which you call up a specific object of mind for inquiry (thought, feeling, event in our lives, and so on). When you do the open meditation, you ask about every thought, feeling, or perception that arises while you sit (a physical pain, for example, or a sound). You ask, "Does this create well-being? Does this create suffering?" Once you have identified where the thought, feeling, or perception leads you, then you can ask, "What is the true nature of this thought/feeling/perception?" (*True nature* means what it consists of.) Remember, although this process is precise and requires attentiveness, it does not call for intellectual analysis. Simply hold the thought or feeling in your mindful attention and see what reveals itself.

Once you feel this process has run its course (for now, at least), you can ask, "Who created this thought/feeling/perception?" Frequently we assume something other than the truth. If, for example, we often say to ourselves, "He has made me angry," then we don't acknowledge that the seed of anger is inside us, and that "he" simply touched that seed and set our own anger going. This is an important and potentially liberating question; it can help you restore control to your mind and realize your correct relationship with those around you. Once you have a clear answer to this question, you can then ask, "Is this thought/feeling/perception all I am?" Sometimes the answer to that question is "Yes," even though you know intellectually that this is not true; or it may be "No, but it certainly seems as though it is right now." Whatever that answer is, don't hide from it. If the answer is anything other than a clear "No," then this particular thought or feeling or perception is one that could consume you and is worth returning to, perhaps at a later time.

When you do the first guided meditation as a closed meditation, you call up a specific thought, feeling, or perception that has been bothering you. Perhaps you find yourself starting with an open version of this meditation, but something has come up spontaneously and you find that the answer to the fourth question is "No, but it seems that it is." You can go back to the second question: "What is the true nature of this thought/feeling/perception?" You can stay with that question until you feel the process has run its course, and then go on to questions three and four. You can return to question two as many times as you need to, perhaps over several days or weeks. You will find that different aspects of the true nature of the thought, feeling, or perception will reveal themselves, and that each new understanding leads to other understandings in an ever widening and deepening spiral.

As always, conscious breathing is our anchor with this guided meditation. When you lose awareness of your breath, you can be pretty sure you have retreated into your analytical thinking or have gone out of your body and into discursive thought. Your conscious breath will bring you back to your mind/heart and solidly into your body.

With chronic thought patterns, feeling-states, or perceptions that create suffering in your life, you can return to the process of this first guided meditation again and again. Each time you do, your relationship with this chronic problem area will shift, perhaps only slightly and only for a moment or two at first, and then more significantly and solidly as the practice sessions go on. You can use this particular guided meditation as a supplement to psychotherapy, as a way of deepening your understanding of your problems and helping you form new, more positive behaviors.

You can also expand this first guided meditation by developing your awareness of the *who* for whom your thought, feeling, or perception may create suffering or well-being. Does this feeling of anger create suffering for my spouse? Does this thought that I have to hoard money or possessions create suffering for someone else who has no food or home? Does my feeling of ease or convenience in buying a phosphate-based dishwashing detergent create suffering for fish and plants in the water where my waste is discharged? When you begin to expand the focus of the question "Does this create well-being or suffering?" you expand your awareness of who you really are. Can I really see myself as separate from my spouse? From my neighbor? From the animals and plants who share the earth with me? In this way, this particular guided meditation can be used as an adjunct to the practice of loving-kindness (or metta) meditation.

The second guided meditation builds on the awareness of thoughts that you developed in the seventh week. Again, the meditation uses judgment thoughts as its subject (although you can substitute any thought pattern or object of concentration you wish), and again and always, you will use conscious breathing as your anchor. Here, rather than focusing on the rising and falling away of the thought, invite yourself to hold steady with the thought and focus your concentration on it. This focus allows you to move more deeply into the heart of your judgment thought and to become one with it. As you do this, you will naturally find that the thought itself starts to shift and change. This shifting and changing is normal, and it is different from discursive thinking. The shift and change is the opening of the judgment thought, the revelation of its true nature. You will know when this happens; the experience of penetrating deeply into the judgment thought is like an "Aha!" experience or an epiphany. The revelation doesn't arise from your analytical mind; instead, it spontaneously arises from your mind/heart as you directly engage yourself with the thought. As your mindfulness grows stronger, compassion naturally arises.

Both guided meditations offer a basic lesson in two realities. One of these the Buddha called "no-self." "Non-self" or "no-self" is greatly misunderstood. It does not mean the denial or annihilation of your body, feelings, thoughts, or consciousness. It tries to express the reality that no part of anything (including you) is separate from anything else in life. Another way to express this is to say that your "self" is made up entirely of things that are not "you" — that is, everything else. Your judgment thoughts are made up of many other components — perhaps fear, loneliness, shame, or isolation. In the first guided meditation, the more frequently you come back to chronic thought, feeling, or perception patterns, the more elements you will find in them; and the more you expand the circle of the *who* for whom your thought, feeling, or perception causes suffering, so will you realize how your own being is made up of the beings of others. Do you recognize the similarity between this investigation and the practices you learned for looking at your food in "Eating Meditation"? Eventually, you will find that the list of things that make up other things has no end. In a very real sense, the entire cosmos lives in that single "object of mind."

The other basic lesson the Buddha called "impermanence." This expresses the reality that nothing, including your "self," remains the same throughout time and space. For example, the thoughts, feelings, and perceptions causing suffering or well-being constantly arise and change, sometimes obviously and sometimes subtly. One day, you realize a particular thought creates well-being; the next, the same thought may recur and you may realize it now creates suffering. At one moment, you may be submerged in suffering; in the next moment, you may regain your equilibrium. The judgment thoughts shift and change as you engage with them. As you practice, you will come to experience that everything in life is like your thoughts and feelings: Everything arises and passes away.

On some level, we all find impermanence and non-self challenging realities. We want the things we love to stay as they are, and we want to have the things we dislike go away permanently. We all have fear of change. The simple guided meditations in this section, and the way in which they open up the experience of non-self and imper-manence, can help you work with this fear, especially when you encounter feelings, thoughts, or perceptions you dislike. You may feel grateful when they fall away, and you may think, "Thank goodness for impermanence." So this is a good place to start.

You will also begin to understand the way non-self and impermanence intersect: Things (and you) exist because different elements have come together at a partic-ular time and place. So long as these elements that sustain something exist, that particular thing will be there. For example, when I was hiking, my perception that it would take a long time for me to get back to my car provided a nutrient to an already existing seed of fear. That nutrient made my fear rise up. The Buddha called these elements "causes and conditions." So long as the appropriate causes and conditions exist, he explained, our perception and the object of our perception will exist. No perception, no object of perception; no object of perception, no perception. This same web of causes and conditions creates the entire world we encounter. Without causes and conditions, things cease to exist, just as a flower withers without sun-light or water or earth. As causes and conditions change, the world changes.

Object of mind meditations can be very powerful and complete. In their deepest form, they not only assist us to discipline our rampaging minds, and thus help us liberate ourselves from the tyranny of our thoughts, feelings, and perceptions; they also open the door to the experience of the realities of no-self and impermanence. When we truly experience non-self and impermanence, our illusion of being separate falls away and we contact the ground of being from which all things arise and pass away. In the "I/you" world in which we live, we encounter the reality of nonduality when we truly experience that we cannot separate ourselves as the perceivers from what we perceive or ourselves as the thinkers from what we are thinking. The personal identification slips away; the fear is at once "my" fear and, simply, fear, part of the common ground of being. In this nondualistic world, the world of mindfulness, there is no "I/my/me," no labeling, no personalizing. Once this door is open, we can simply be present in mindfulness, aware of what is going on, and even for brief moments, as we experience the nonduality inside our dualistic world, not even being aware that we are aware. In Zen, this experience of mindfulness is expressed: "In the seeing, only what is seen. In the hearing, only what is heard. In the touching, only what is touched. In the feeling, only what is felt. In the thinking, only what is thought."

When we "get" the reality of all this in our being, we encounter life as it is. I have noticed that those who truly have lived this awareness, even if only for a moment, soften a bit around the edges. In my own life, my experience of this has helped me open my heart and be more loving, kind, understanding, and compassionate. For me, it is very simple: Everything makes up me, I am part of everything. I am the result of causes and conditions that I and countless others create, and I create causes and conditions for myself and countless others. I know that all things change when causes and conditions change, and that brings up the desire to make as many as I can of these causes and conditions ones that promote peace and love. To manifest this in my daily life, I must cultivate the space and activity of mindfulness, where the words, and my own personal narrative, drop away. This lies deep at the heart of the Buddha's teachings on mindfulness. Here we can touch life directly, outside of notions, concepts, and beliefs. Here we can embrace the heart of the cosmos.

MINDFUL CONVERSATION

One of the basic mindfulness practices I use in my classes involves conversation. Each class has a period at the end where we engage in dialogue. Each of us has the opportunity to talk about what is happening in our practice and to get suggestions and support. This is as much a mindfulness practice as the sitting and walking meditation we've done that day; the thread of mindfulness remains unbroken as we move into the practices of mindful speech and deep listening, the practice of mindful conversation.

We have many ways of being with one another, but conversation is one of the most meaningful. Through our words we exchange information and we learn about each other. We humans tend to be language-based. Most of us think in words and in the concepts that words express. As you deepen your practice of mindfulness and become more aware of the consequences of your actions, you will also discover the deep impact that your words have on yourself and others. We know from our lives and encounters that words can make us feel great or lousy. We've all spoken rashly and regretted it later (or sometimes immediately), and we've all been on the receiving end of angry or hurtful words and have felt the impact they had on us. Most of us have also encountered someone who listened to us with such understanding that we felt better just from talking.

Mindfulness can help make our conversations deeper, more meaningful, more satisfying. To get to that point, just as with everything else, we first have to walk through our ideas of what conversation ought to be.

I divide mindful conversation into two parts: mindful speech and deep listening. You have perhaps encountered these words elsewhere in other contexts. I ask you to put aside your preconceptions about what they mean as you continue with this section. You will develop your own understanding.

Mindful Speech

When I was in high school, my English teacher had a favorite phrase: "Be sure mind is engaged before putting mouth into gear." That nugget describes the first aspect of mindful speech: Be aware of what you are saying while you say it. Many of us express our anxiety and discomfort in social situations through mindless speech. We ramble and prattle on without any real awareness of what we are saying — we're filling up space, filling the void of our fear and anxiety with words. Sometimes I even talk to myself when I'm alone (do you?). You may not even know what drives your unmindful speech, and perhaps you feel like you can't control it. How can you enact my English teacher's clear and wise direction?

The first step, as always, is to become aware of your

breathing and of what feelings or thoughts are passing through you. This can be an instantaneous process of recognition, and just by doing that you may already calm down and the urge to speak mindlessly may pass. Once you have encountered the reality of how you are feeling and thinking, then you can express yourself honestly and clearly. Use the guided meditation question from the eighth week: Will my speech create suffering or well-being for myself and for others? Here are some basic suggestions that I encourage myself and my students to follow both in our weekly classes and in daily life:

- Focus on your own feelings and thoughts, not someone else's. Speak your truth. Don't parrot what you've heard or read, and don't try to speak for someone else, even if it's your spouse, child, or parent.

- Be aware of the impact of your words on the other person. There are always different ways to express yourself. Being honest does not mean being hurtful. Being mindful does not always mean being nice. Check in with yourself: Are you trying to make the other person responsible for your feelings or for fixing your situation through your words? If you are, be careful, because the other person is not likely to hear you.

- Speak from the reality of your life, not from concepts or ideas (unless, of course, you're discussing concepts and ideas).

- Avoid melodrama and generalization. "You always do this" or "I never get that" cover over pain or anger. Become aware of the pain or anger, or whatever is going on for you, and

then tell the person honestly and compassionately what
you are feeling. "Right now I am upset because I don't feel
heard" is a more mindful expression of reality than "You
never listen to me." Consider which of those sentences
you would respond well to, and speak accordingly.

- Remember that mindfulness means staying in the present moment, not being pulled into the past or launching
off into the future. Speak about the present reality.

- Share the best of yourself through your words — your
joy, your love, your anguish. Try to avoid sharing the
worst of yourself — your blaming, criticizing, and judgmental words. Try to use your words to support rather
than to tear down.

Deep Listening

There is a big difference between hearing someone and listening to someone. Hearing is something we do with our
ears: I can be hearing you talk and be doing something
completely different. I may nod at the appropriate points
and even say, "I hear you." But do you really feel as though
I've listened to you if my attention is somewhere else?
What if I stop what I'm doing and put all of my attention
on you? What if I keep myself focused on you and not on
my agenda or the next activity in my life? Which way
would you prefer to have a conversation with me?

Deep listening means listening with our entire being,
not just our ears or even just our ears and our intellect.
Try this: The next time you have a conversation with your
best friend, see if you can simply listen without interrupt-
ing. Can you listen without judging her or even reacting to

what she is saying? Most of the time, we are concerned not just with what the other person is saying, but also with our response to it. We may wonder, "How would I react in that situation?" Or we may think, "I can fix that," and begin to offer suggestions. Have you noticed that once you begin to offer suggestions, the other person seems disappointed or a bit turned off? That's because the "fix-it" suggestion isn't what the other person really needs. What he needs, simply, is to be listened to.

Here are some guidelines for deep listening:

- Listen calmly. Let the other person speak without interruption.

- Let the other person know you are truly interested in what he has to say by asking questions instead of offering suggestions. Share your experiences only if they are relevant. Offer advice only when asked.

- Do your best not to think about what you will say when it is your time to speak. The clever and helpful things that come up in response to someone else's enthusiasms, delights, or suffering distract us all. These can distract you from paying complete attention to what you are hearing.

- Listen with the full depth of your mindfulness. Much of what the other person is trying to communicate to you might be in what is left unsaid. Listen to what is inside and underneath the words.

- Keep yourself as open and accepting as possible. We all notice other people's tendency to judge us, and once we feel judged we become defensive and close down.

Mindful conversation is a practice you can use many times each day. Every time you talk with someone at work, employ mindful conversation. Listen closely and without judgment, speak clearly, acknowledge the other person, and be honest and truthful. For more suggestions, I strongly recommend Marshall Rosenberg's work in nonviolent communication. His suggestions about how to approach human interaction help to make mindful conversation a living reality. His book *Nonviolent Communication* is available on his website, www.cnvc.org, as are many suggestions for mindful conversation and information about his nonviolent communication training program.

HOME PLAY

FORMAL PRACTICE: Every other day, do the first guided meditation. On the alternate days, allow yourself to build stability in your sitting meditation practice by engaging mindfully with thoughts and feelings as they arise. As you encounter thoughts and feelings, use the skills you have learned from the guided meditations on the body, feelings, and thinking to help you engage mindfully in the present moment and give your meditation some direction.

INFORMAL PRACTICE: Continue telephone and red light meditation. Do your best to make any occasion of your day an opportunity to practice mindfulness. When you are conversing with someone, engage in mindful conversation, and when you are listening to him or her especially do your best to not think of what you will say next. Try doing this for one conversation each day at first. Over time, you can expand this to encompass most of your conversations with one or two of your friends or loved ones, and then eventually to all of your conversations. Please be realistic: This is a challenging practice. Be forgiving with yourself when your old habits get in your way. Keep your attention on just listening. Consider whether you have heard your friend differently. Notice how your interaction with your friend has changed because of this.

PART THREE

WIDENING
THE HEART

PRACTICING
LOVING-KINDNESS

When I began mindfulness practice many years ago, I picked up a few little books in Thailand to help me along. The Thais have published many free pamphlets to help people establish mindfulness practice, and I chose ones that offered the basics. In one of them the author wrote about the importance of cultivating a "pure mind." He offered this image: The pure mind is a beautiful, clean, white room in which there are five doors; these doors open to the worlds of form, feeling, perception, mental formations, and consciousness. The goal of cultivating a pure mind, he wrote, is not to let anything from these five worlds come in through the doors and dirty up the beautiful white room. The author also wrote a great deal about "defilements" and offered the practice of cultivating a pure mind as the way to rid ourselves of these defilements and attain awakening. This pure-mind teaching is an important part of one particular mindfulness tradition.

These little books from Thailand were not especially well translated into English, and I am sure the author did not intend me to take his instructions as I did. I began doing sitting meditation every day, sometimes for up to two hours without stopping, focused entirely on the rising and falling of my breath. I would continue sitting until I became aware only of my breathing, and awareness of the activities of my mind would seem to disappear. I thought I was attaining a pure mind. This kind of sitting meditation was my whole practice, and it became the center of my life. I put this practice above everything, and I would frequently get to work late and mess up arrangements I had made with other people because I did not want to stop sitting. And no matter how "pure" my mind was while I was sitting, the same difficult thoughts and feelings came up in daily life and I still didn't know how to handle them. My practice might have looked good on the outside, but the reality of my life was messy. I didn't realize it at the time, but sitting practice was a great escape.

Several years later I attended my first Zen meditation retreat with my first Zen teacher, the wonderful Zen Master Su Bong. At that time he had not received his Zen master ordination and he was called by his monk's name, Mu Deung Sunim. While I had had intermittent contact with Buddhist monks and asked basic questions about practice, I had never had an "interview" with a Zen teacher. I had heard a lot about them — the shouting, the challenges of Zen riddles (koans), and so forth — but I had no real sense of what to expect.

So I walked into my first interview with Mu Deung. After he motioned me to sit on a cushion facing him, he asked my name and then asked what kind of practice I had been doing. I described to him my sitting meditation practice, that "pure mind" cultivation. He then said, "Well, that's wonderful. But you could sit like that with your eyes closed for ten thousand years and never save one being from suffering!"

I felt as though Mu Deung had thrown a pail of very cold water on my face. He had seen right through me and had offered me my first koan, my first challenge in practice. But what had he seen?

Like all good teachers, Mu Deung had opened a door for me that had many different levels of meaning. He taught me that a clear mind that can handle both the "pure" and the "impure" is more valuable in daily life than a "pure mind." He also understood that I was using my meditation practice as a way of reinforcing my sense of separateness from the world. I was too focused on my-self as a separate being and I was using practice to escape from my life. I was a full-time lawyer in those days, and Mu Deung saw that even though I did good works for people, I didn't understand the interconnectedness of the suffering and well-being of my clients and me. I practiced as though my sitting meditation, my "pure mind," and I lived in isolation.

That sense of isolation, as I found out, is something just about all of us have. Many teachers from many different traditions have seen this as the core of human suffer-ing. The great poet Rumi wrote vividly of his feelings of loneliness and isolation from "the beloved"; Christian and Jewish writers speak of "hell" as "separation from God." In the Buddhist world, every teaching points us in the direction of realizing that the reality of life is what Thich Nhat Hanh calls "interbeing," the profound and inescapable interconnectedness of all beings and all phenomena. Without this awareness, we can end up where I was headed, developing a "pure mind" in isolation, trying to be the classic "holy man" on a mountaintop. What happens when I encounter the rest of the world in daily life? Or as Mu Deung suggested, can I offer the balm of peacefulness and human recognition to even one person?

Until now, you have focused the attention of your practice on two areas: establishing the habits and practices of mindfulness in your daily life and developing greater understanding of your mind and your own self. If your experience is like mine, or like those of my students, you have already experienced the transformative power of mindfulness. You have also most likely experienced that the transformation does not only happen to you. Mindfulness helps transform our relationships with one another, and we can see the impact of our mindfulness practice on our relationships with our families, friends, co-workers, and others.

Another way of transforming relationships through mindfulness involves changing your focus to include the reality of interbeing. Instead of focusing only on your own being, you put your focus on yourself and on others at the same time. Wish yourself and others well, or offer the stability and well-being that you nourish in your mindfulness practice to help others heal. Those of us who have been raised in the Western Judeo-Christian context may recognize similar instructions from our root traditions, whether it is the Jewish imperative of *tikkun o'lam* ("heal the world") or the Christian exhortation to charity. In mindfulness practice, too, we learn to nourish our own well-being and heal our own suffering by bearing witness to the suffering of others and nourishing their well-being.

Mu Deung was offering to assist me in taking the first real steps toward living the reality of interbeing. It is important to make this reality more than simply a concept to be explored, to make it alive and vital in your life. By "vital," I mean something that you live in your being and in your daily life. The living and vital "clear mind" that lives the reality of interbeing is always there: It is your intuitive sense of what to do and what not to do in every situation; it is your spontaneous wisdom; it is your open and loving heart that can meet each person with respect and recognition.

In our last weeks together, I offer two practices to help you create this living, vital awareness of interbeing by breaking down the barriers between others and yourself. These two practices come from different traditions. One goes by the name *metta* or "loving-kindness" practice and comes from one of the early talks by the Buddha; the other goes by the name *tonglin* and comes from the Tibetan tradition. We'll explore tonglin in the next chapter.

These practices widen our hearts. Doing them helps us to cultivate love and compassion for others and ourselves. Many teachers offer instruction in these practices in great depth. Many practitioners make these practices their lifetime's work. I am not a metta or tonglin specialist. What I offer here is the most basic of introductions.

Metta:
The Practice of Loving-Kindness

Offering loving-kindness to myself:

May I be well and happy.
May I be strong, confident, and peaceful.
May I have ease and well-being.

Offering loving-kindness to a neutral person; to someone I like; to someone I love; and to someone I hate:

May you be well and happy.
May you be strong, confident, and peaceful.
May you have ease and well-being.

Metta practice uses a carefully structured series of guided meditations to help us nourish loving-kindness in ourselves and in our relationships. The phrases used in these guided meditations have many different translations, so if you have read books on metta by Sharon Salzberg or others, my version here may look different. The practice also has at least two different structures, and you may find that another author uses one that differs from mine. In my experience, the precise words of the phrases and the structure of the practice are not as important as the intent.

The way that I learned metta meditation involves at least a five-stage process. You offer loving-kindness first to yourself; then to a person about whom you feel neutral; then to a person whom you like; then to a person whom you love dearly; and finally to a person about whom you have strong negative feelings like hatred or terror. These five groupings encompass our relationships with all of the living beings in the world. By going through the process of metta meditation, you will understand your relationships and yourself better, and you will expand your heart to encompass with loving-kindness both the people and feelings you most love and those you most despise.

As with all of the guided meditations you have done so far, metta meditation is a guiding North Star. Using metta phrases is not intended to make you "force" love; it is intended to bring you face to face with where you are now so you can offer loving-kindness to your own suffering and the suffering of others. When I point myself in the direction of offering loving-kindness, what comes up? I encounter my obstacles at the same time as I cultivate loving-kindness. That is the point of this practice. When you are in touch with what comes up, and at the same time maintain the direction of metta, you can enter so deeply into your own anguish that you can emerge from it with your perspective transformed and your heart widened. That is when you can truly embrace your suffering and the suffering of others with love. That is also when you realize that your suffering is no different from the suffering of others, for every attitude we have toward another person is an attitude we have toward ourselves. If we hate someone, it is because we hate those same feelings and tendencies in ourselves. If we judge someone, it is because we judge ourselves in the same way. So we offer loving-kindness to ourselves and to others, and in the process the walls begin to soften and the heart opens.

Metta practice is usually done in sitting meditation. Begin as always by becoming aware of your in-breath and out-breath, and ground yourself in your breath in the way that you learned in the fourth week. Once you are established in your breathing, which should take a few minutes, say these lines to yourself:

May I be well and happy.
May I be strong, confident, and peaceful.
May I have ease and well-being.

Breathe in and out, repeat these phrases to yourself to help you set the direction for your practice, and see what happens. When you say, "May I be well and happy," do you feel well and happy or do you suddenly become aware of a pain in your legs, or do you perhaps find feelings of unworthiness or low self-esteem rising up? When we continue to practice in the direction of metta and allow ourselves to be completely present to the pain in our legs, we are offering wellness and happiness to our pain. What happens then? Does the pain get worse or better? What thoughts or feelings come up? Do we feel, perhaps, hopelessness that the pain will ever abate? Continue to practice this way and see where you go, always using metta as your North Star. You may drop away the repetition of the phrases, but if you do, make the effort to maintain the direction of offering wellness and happiness to yourself. As always, conscious breathing is your anchor. Maintaining an awareness of your in- and out-breaths in your body as you go through the metta process will help you stay grounded in your practice.

Sometimes you may want to use all three phrases

together, like a gatha. Sometimes you may want to use only one line of a phrase or sometimes one word. If you have particular difficulty with confidence, you may get many fruitful minutes (or hours) of practice just saying, "May I be confident." In my experience, however, it is important to encompass the full range of metta intention in practice rather than to isolate one segment.

Once you have offered loving-kindness to yourself in this way, proceed to offer it to others. Metta practice uses a particular order for doing this. First, offer loving-kindness to someone for whom you have relatively neutral feelings; then to someone you like; then to someone you love dearly; and then to someone you hate. This order is important. While it may seem easier to offer loving-kindness to someone you love dearly, your attachments to that person can get in the way. Instead of offering loving-kindness freely, you may find yourself offering it with conditions: I want her to be happy *with me,* I want him to be confident *but not so much that he'll leave his secure job,* and so on. It is easier to offer loving-kindness first to someone to whom you aren't attached or averse. Once you can do that with sincerity and openness, you can go on to the more intimate, and troublesome, relationships.

In my class we do metta in an introductory fashion and combine all five aspects of the practice into one sitting meditation session of thirty-five minutes. This is helpful as an overview and as a way to start the practice, and sometimes it can help establish an attitude of loving-kindness for the day. To do metta as a deeply transformative practice, however, it is more helpful to do the five aspects in stages, perhaps one per day or even one per week.

After you have offered loving-kindness to yourself, offer it to someone for whom you have neutral feelings, that is, someone to whom you are not strongly attached nor averse. Someone you don't know very well might be a good person to start with, like the bank teller or checkout person at the market whom you saw today. Use the same phrases and just change the pronouns:

May (s)he be well and happy.
May (s)he be strong, confident, and peaceful.
May (s)he have ease and well-being.

Again, as you do this, see what comes up. Can you offer this loving-kindness genuinely, or are you trying to force it? Can you perhaps offer this to people you don't know, like those who suffer from drought or malnutrition or those who live in war zones? Can you offer this to the homeless person you saw this morning on the street? What thoughts or feelings come up when you do? Continue to follow the process of your mind, not by intellectual analysis and not by distanced observation, but by being present with the thoughts and feelings and holding your metta direction.

Now offer loving-kindness to someone you like. "Like" is not the same as "love dearly." A friend may be a good person to start with. As you move closer in intimacy, what kinds of thoughts and feelings come up? Do you find yourself visualizing more detailed outcomes for your friend? Do you find attachments rising up? Again, follow what happens and hold the metta direction.

Now offer loving-kindness to someone you love dearly,

such as a spouse, child, parent, or another dear one. Our relationships with those we love dearly are more complex. Here we meet with our expectations and disappointments, our attachments and desires, a lot more clearly. Depending on what day it is, or even what time of day, and what your last interaction with this beloved person was, you may even find that offering loving-kindness is the last thing you want to do! He made me so angry this morning, why should I wish *him* well?!? Some of what you discover about your feelings toward those you love may surprise you. Can I really love my spouse without attachments? For me, the answer is "Sometimes." As I begin to see what is getting in the way of my offering of loving-kindness, I can feel a transformation happen: I want so much to love this person well, I can feel my disappointment in myself and my frustration with my anxiety, fear, and desire. As I embrace all of these thoughts and feelings, the doorway opens and loving-kindness just happens. My relationship to myself and to the one I love is transformed.

The same process I've described for one we love applies in spades to someone we hate. In class I am fortunate to have people honest enough to ask why they should ever want to offer loving-kindness to someone they loathe. I can give an answer based on my experience: Everything I hate in others is something I hate in myself, and my hatred warps my life and causes me and others great pain. However, the very best answer I can give is, "Try it." Inevitably the first reaction is a desire to avoid: We either have difficulty maintaining our attention on the person we hate or we feel an intense desire to get up and leave the room. Do your best to stay focused on your discomfort and to return your attention to your breathing and to the person you hate and say, "May (s)he be well and happy." What comes up? "No, I want that person to suffer, and suffer big; I want him to feel so much pain he'll never hurt another person in his life!" Enter into that feeling. A good way to do that, I find, is to ask, "Who is suffering?" Aren't both of us? Aren't our sufferings interconnected? Do I want to break the cycle of suffering? Or perhaps you can combine metta with the guided meditation on objects of mind and ask, "Does this thought create suffering or well-being?" Inevitably you will find that you have created much of the suffering yourself in your own mind.

Metta is a practice of focusing on the stars and spending time in the sewer simultaneously. When we offer kindness, if we are honest we get to see how unkind we are. Only by embracing your unkindness can you be kind; only by spending time in the sewer can you find your way out.

You can also use the metta phrases as a way to establish a direction or intention for your daily-life mindfulness. When you wake in the morning, say to yourself, for example, "May all beings be peaceful," or "May all beings have ease and well-being." You can then repeat the phrase to yourself over again throughout the day, so that no matter what you are doing, the metta phrase is going on in the background of your consciousness. This has a subtle and long-lasting effect, because repeating the phrase over again like this allows it to enter deep into your consciousness and helps you to release your wellspring of lovingkindness. As always, when you establish a direction in daily life, you become aware of what stands in your way. So, when you establish the direction "May all beings be peaceful," you may become acutely aware of how much the beings you meet (including yourself) are not peaceful. In this situation, metta allows us to offer something to the nonpeacefulness we encounter: our wish and desire that we, and everyone else, experience peace in our lives. We hold the reality of our lives and the intention to improve our lives and the lives of everyone at the same time. This can be a powerful and transformative practice.

This introduction to metta is very basic. If you want to pursue this practice, please read some of the great books that have been written on the subject by Sharon Salzberg, the Dalai Lama, Thich Nhat Hanh, and others. To get the full impact, do a workshop with a teacher who specializes in teaching metta practice, such as Sharon Salzberg or Daeja Napier.

Home Play

FORMAL PRACTICE: Try incorporating metta practice into your daily sitting meditation. See what happens to your capacity to handle difficult states of mind in your sitting or walking practice when you offer metta to yourself. Find one person with whom you have a difficult time, and try focusing your metta practice on that person. See how your relationship to that person changes over the week as you practice.

INFORMAL PRACTICE: Take "metta breaks" during the day, perhaps during your walking meditation during lunch or at a quiet moment at your work or at home. When you are with someone whom you find problematic, see if you can offer metta to him or her silently while you are in his or her presence. Try to incorporate the intention of metta into your listening: Listen with your heart and mind, not just your ears.

PRACTICING
COMPASSION

TONGLIN: THE PRACTICE OF COMPASSION

- Establish mindful breathing and the awareness of the space that expands and contracts with each in and out breath.

- Become aware of breathing as exchange: Air from inside is being exchanged with air from outside, and vice versa.

- Become aware of the nature of exchange: always reciprocal and mutually sustaining.

- Offer healing to a specific person by breathing in their suffering and breathing out healing.

- Expand the range of healing to all people who have the same kind of suffering.

One of the members of my meditation community in Maynard, Massachusetts, introduced me to tonglin and it rapidly became one of my favorite practices. As you might have gathered, I prefer practices that put me at the edge of the cliff and don't give me room to wriggle out. My mind is so good at avoiding that I appreciate and benefit most from practices that hold my feet to the fire. Tonglin is one of those practices.

Tonglin practice is rooted in the breath. If you can breathe in and out, you can practice tonglin. Tonglin works with a sense of breathing that may be foreign to you at first, because it sees the in-breath as drawing in and the out-breath as opening up. You may tend to see the in-breath as expansive, because your lungs expand and because you have a natural feeling of spaciousness, and you may see the out-breath as contracting because your lungs contract. To get the experience of how tonglin works with the breath, try this: Take an in-breath with awareness that you are bringing all of the energy from outside yourself and inside yourself into one concentrated point in your lungs. Then, let your out-breath happen with awareness that you are allowing all of that energy to flow expansively outward, through all the cells in your body and out into the world around you. Once you have tried this a few times, you may find, as I have, that it becomes a natural way to experience breathing.

Tonglin is very direct. The essence of the practice is to breathe in the suffering of another person and to breathe out loving-kindness, compassion, and healing. All of us have reference points for pain, and for joy and healing, in our lives; we can practice breathing in suffering and breathing out healing because we know that both exist. When I describe it this way, many of my students' first reaction is, "Won't someone else's suffering contaminate me? Shouldn't I be breathing my own suffering out? What if the suffering I breathe in overwhelms me? What if I don't have any healing energy to offer?" In fact, tonglin is balanced: We do not drown in suffering because tonglin constantly reminds us to breathe out healing; we do not hide in false joy because tonglin constantly reminds us to breathe in suffering. We receive and we give.

In tonglin practice, we think of a person we know who is suffering and whom we want to help. Perhaps we visualize that person in front of us. We can see or sense their suffering. And we breathe in. We offer to take that suffering into our own being, trusting that the resources for healing are inside of us. And we breathe that healing out, making our offering to the other person. We are making the greatest gift we can, the gift of our loving and healing energy, to help relieve another's suffering. As you breathe in suffering and breathe out healing, you will find quite naturally that compassion arises. This is because a compassionate response to suffering is to offer some help. In tonglin, awareness of suffering and compassionate action are inextricably linked together.

The questions my students raise come from their fears, and you may find that you share them. Tonglin taps into the reality that when we focus on the suffering of another person, our own suffering also surfaces. Frequently, the suffering we encounter in ourselves is the same as that of the person we are offering to help. For example, my first wife died in 1982, and when I offer to breathe in the suffering of someone who has lost a spouse or other family member, what I first encounter are my own feelings about Sara's death. Tonglin helps me to realize that what causes others to suffer is the same as what causes me to suffer. And once I touch the tenderness and beauty, and the grief and helplessness, I feel from Sara's death, those feelings extend to the other person who has suffered a loss and for whom I'm doing the tonglin.

At other times, the suffering we encounter is not so directly related. I have encountered powerlessness, hopelessness, feeling overwhelmed, and at times just being stuck. When these feelings are present, the suffering I encounter may seem more than I can handle. We always start where we are, so at those times I have begun by offering healing to myself for the piece of suffering that is right in my face. But as I breathe in this suffering, I also allow myself to breathe in all of the powerlessness, hopelessness, or overwhelmed stuckness of everyone else. That is the spirit of tonglin, recognizing that we are not separate, that our suffering is not separate. If we are to benefit, it is because everyone benefits, and vice versa. It's more important that I locate the feelings in my body than label them, so I dive into my churning stomach or aching back and I breathe in everyone's churning stomach or aching back. Then I breathe out the calm, stability, and serenity to heal it. In this direct way, I encourage myself to drop the barrier of separation and isolation.

Occasionally I feel as though I cannot find what will heal the suffering I've encountered. When this happens, I first become aware of my breathing and then of the feelings that are going on. Am I panicked or worried? I breathe in with panic or worry, and with some realization that others in the world are also panicked or worried. Then I breathe out with compassion for the panic or worry — not just mine, but others' as well. The most important thing is to be present to the panic, to breathe in with everyone in the world who experiences panic, and to breathe out with compassion and with relief that we are not alone.

When you want to help someone who is suffering and you begin tonglin, perhaps you will find yourself worried that you'll drown in your friend's suffering. Try to breathe in the worry of everyone in the world and breathe out whatever will heal that worry. Do this for ten or fifteen minutes and see what happens.

We don't do tonglin just for another person or just for ourselves, because tonglin makes real for us the lack of separateness of "self" and "other." Because we are breathing in the suffering of another, our own suffering gets triggered. Because we are breathing out healing for another, we heal ourselves. Remember Mu Deung's koan for me: "You could sit with your eyes closed for ten thousand years and never save one being from suffering"? Tonglin becomes the living embodiment of the answer. Tonglin also taps into something powerful that most spiritual traditions acknowledge: We help to alleviate our own suffering when we help to alleviate the suffering of others. My wife Avril's first meditation teacher, Baba Muktananda, would frequently tell people who came to him and complained of the woes in their lives, "Go and do something good for someone else." Tonglin is a concrete way of offering healing to others and healing ourselves at the same time.

As I practice tonglin, the barriers dissolve and the weight of suffering becomes much less. At first, what I experience is that I am no longer suffering in isolation; we are all in it together. Then, as I continue to breathe in the suffering or pain, all ownership of that suffering or pain begins to dissipate. It's not my suffering, and it isn't the other person's suffering either. It's just suffering, part of the condition of human consciousness. Tonglin is described as the practice of "exchanging self and other." This isn't simply putting ourselves in another person's situation. It's acknowledging, and experiencing as a living reality, the existence of suffering and the existence of healing, compassion, and loving-kindness in human consciousness. The suffering and healing don't belong to me, and they don't belong to you; they belong to all of us.

When I practice tonglin for someone who is dying or someone who is mourning the death of a loved one and my recollection of Sara's death comes up, the experience of having someone die and the feelings that go with it become something universal. There is endless death, endless sadness, endless love and compassion — not mine, not his or hers. The experience is ours, it's part of all of us, it comes up when the conditions are right for it to come up, and it goes away when the conditions are right for it to leave. And that, ultimately, is the reality of this thing we call our "self": a succession of thoughts, feelings, and perceptions that we all somehow share in common.

While tonglin is traditionally done as a sitting meditation practice, I have found that I use it frequently during the day. When I am at work and see people with a lot of hurt, anger, or difficulty, I will take a moment or two to practice tonglin for them and for myself. I find tonglin a versatile practice. Tonglin traditionally has four stages. When I use the practice myself, I divide up one of those stages, making six, and I suggest trying this way of guiding yourself:

- Become aware of your breathing and allow yourself and your breath to come to a place of rest. Bring your breath into your body, and become aware of the spaciousness each in-breath opens in your body, and of the movement of breath and energy each out-breath creates. Ground your breath in your body as you learned to do in the fourth week.

- Become aware of breathing as a process of exchange. Allow yourself on every in-breath to be aware of air coming from a huge ocean of air that surrounds you, down the river of your nose and breathing tubes into the lake of your lungs and abdomen. Allow yourself on every out-breath to sense the air going from the lake in your lungs and abdomen back up the river and out into the ocean of air surrounding you.

- Become aware of the nature of exchange: It is always reciprocal and mutually sustaining. I use a plant as a focus point for this. The air I breathe in contains oxygen, which the plant produces and which I need to live. The air I breathe out contains carbon dioxide, which my body produces and which the plant needs to live.

- Allow your awareness of your breathing to move into your heart-space. This is the area in the center of your chest at the same level where your heart is. Notice any sadness, pain, or difficulty that you are experiencing. Breathe in your sadness, pain, or difficulty, and as you breathe out, offer love and compassion, to yourself from your heart.

- Now begin working with the person and situation to which you want to offer healing. Step out of your heart-space and return to awareness of your breath coming in through your nose, going down the river of your breathing apparatus to the lake of your belly, and then back up the river to the ocean of air surrounding you. Breathe in the other's suffering and breathe out loving-kindness, compassion, and healing. Don't hold the suffering inside. Let the natural process of breathing — the passage of air from your nose to your belly and back again, looping through your heart-space — transform the suffering into love and compassion, and move it out. If your own problems stand in your way, then work first with whatever comes up for you; breathe in that feeling, thought, or sensation not only for yourself but also for all people who feel the same thing. Do your best to maintain awareness of how your suffering and the other person's or people's suffering intersect.

- Expand your scope. Instead of breathing in the suffering of one friend, breathe in the suffering of all people in the same situation. If your friend has AIDS, breathe in the suffering of everyone who has AIDS. If your friend is going through a divorce, breathe in the suffering of everyone who has endured the wrenching coming-apart of an intimate relationship. If you are working with your own feelings, then try bringing some metta perspective into the practice. If you are working with anxiety, see what happens if you breathe in to heal the anxiety of someone who has made you suffer. If you can do tonglin for them too, you'll see that they have the same anxiety inside themselves that you do. Maintain your awareness of your own feelings that come up when you do this.

Tonglin practice is not about escape. It is also not about pretense. We only do what we can. Each session offers us the opportunity to expand our awareness of suffering in the world and to offer something positive to help. Each session helps us melt a little more the illusion that we are separate. Tonglin embodies Muktananda's teaching: In offering to help another, we help ourselves. In the face of great pain and suffering, we have something to offer. We can "exchange self and other" (as the teacher Lama Surya Das puts it) and even if only momentarily, tap into the great well of healing and suffering that arises and passes away in the vastness of human consciousness.

In a very practical way, I find that tonglin is a perfect practice for the times when I am listening to someone in a tough position in his or her life. It helps me to bear witness to that suffering. As I listen, I breathe in the pain and anguish; as I breathe out, I offer compassion and healing. I find this helps me to stay present with the other person and to listen more attentively.

When I started doing my version of tonglin practice, I found that I would frequently carry the subject of my practice around with me afterward. The symptom: thoughts about him or her would come up unbidden, or I would have feelings that had nothing to do with my life or experiences. It's not healthy for us to stay connected to someone in that way because we can get confused about whose thoughts or feelings we are experiencing. This can lead us

168 BEGINNING MINDFULNESS

to act in unconscious ways. To prevent this from happening, I make it a point to "disconnect" after practice: I say good-bye consciously, and I do it as many times as is necessary. I encourage you to do the same.

Tonglin is a practice from the Tibetan tradition. Of the teachers writing on tonglin, I particularly suggest reading the works of Pema Chödrön.

The more you do tonglin and metta, the more your relationships with everyone (and everything) around you will change. Metta cultivates the heart of loving-kindness, and tonglin cultivates the heart of compassion. They take us through our own world and show us how much our world and the world of others are interlaced. In fact, those worlds are inseparable. Our situations may be different, and the precise manifestation of our suffering may be different, but our feelings, desires, thoughts, and aspirations are the same. Metta and tonglin focus our attention on real people and real situations, and they encourage us to bear witness to the pain and joy in the life of the world. They encourage us to practice nonseparation, to develop our understanding that the well-being of everyone and everything in the universe is part of our own well-being. Compassion and loving-kindness both spring from and nourish this understanding. Once this understanding stops being a concept in our mind and becomes a living reality, our lives change. In my experience, longtime practitioners of metta and tonglin soften around the edges, and those who encounter them feel seen, heard, and deeply recognized. In two parts of the last section of this book, "Transforming Suffering" and "The Five Mindfulness Trainings," we will explore more fully what living with this understanding means.

These two wonderful practices help us expand the horizon of our awareness. Ultimately they lead us to the experience that Zen Master Seung Sahn calls "not one and not two." We are, each of us, an individual manifestation of something that is not individual at all. Our thoughts, feelings, perceptions, and sensations endlessly arise and fall away, they belong to us and they don't belong to us, and at any given moment you and I, this book, the chair you're sitting on, and the weather outside are perfect and necessary expressions of the cosmos. Tonglin reminds us that, if we want to experience the ultimate reality, we have to experience it in the here and now of our physical reality. If we want to find the ecstasy, we'll find it *in* the laundry!

HOME PLAY

FORMAL PRACTICE: Try switching from metta to tonglin practice in your daily sitting and walking meditation. Observe the differences between how metta and tonglin work for you. Find another person with whom you have a hard time; see if you can locate the suffering that causes him or her to act the way he or she does toward you, and see if you can offer tonglin healing for his or her suffering. See how your relationship with that person changes over the week. See whether you can extend tonglin to a difficult situation in the world (such as an area where there is much tension and conflict); see what feelings this brings up for you and how tonglin works with that.

INFORMAL PRACTICE: Take tonglin breaks during the day just as you took metta breaks in the ninth week. Incorporate the intention of tonglin into your mindful speech and deep listening. See what difference it makes to you and to the other person if you listen with attentiveness and with the intention to offer healing to that person just through your listening presence. Try speaking with honesty and with the awareness of how your words can help to create true healing in the situation you are in.

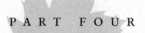

PART FOUR

GOING ON

How to Continue

Congratulations! You've just completed ten weeks (at least) of training in mindfulness. During this time, you have begun to develop some of the habits of mindful living, including mindful eating and mindful walking, and you have begun to develop the habit of doing sitting and walking meditation daily. You have begun the exploration of the nature of your mind. You have found ways to explore how mindfulness manifests itself in the physical world and in the worlds of feeling and thought, and how to widen your heart and enrich your life through the practices of loving-kindness and compassion.

This is a great beginning. The path of mindfulness continues and can lead you more deeply into a vibrant and fulfilling life. Here are some suggestions for continuing.

• Use the guided meditations to help build and consolidate your sitting meditation tools, as well as to encourage transformation and healing. You will find many more guided meditations in Thich Nhat Hanh's book, *The Blooming of a Lotus* (see "Recommended Reading").

- Alternate guided meditations with open sitting practice, during which you simply allow yourself to be aware of your breathing and what is going on inside and around you. This kind of practice allows us to be guided from an inner source and yields wonderful, unexpected results.

- Please try not to get entangled in expectations. Just because you are easily mindful of turning on the light one day does not mean it will be exactly the same the next. One trap to look out for is trying to recapture an experience or feeling you had the last time you sat (or walked or whatever). Go with the experience you are having now, even if it seems hopelessly confused or painful. That is your present reality.

- When in doubt, go back to basics. Remember your breath is your anchor, and simple, honest mindfulness of breathing can lead you right back to the present moment. Don't get caught up in technique. Remember that the instructions and techniques, and even the words of great teachers, are no more than a finger pointing at the moon: Always go for the moon.

- Continue to be regular and disciplined in your formal and informal practices, and continue to be compassionate and forgiving with yourself when you aren't.

- The practices in the first part of this book help to establish stability. The practices in the second and third parts develop further the exploration of the nature of our minds and reality, and help us to stay in touch with our suffering while cultivating positive qualities. Don't be afraid to go back to the practices you have learned in the first part of this book when you feel you need more work on stability. Stability and faith in the practices are necessary before you go on to the more developed formal practices, such as metta and tonglin, or some of the deeper practices of the vipassana, Zen, or Tibetan traditions.

• Find a group to practice with if you don't have one already. I can't say enough about the importance of the group in supporting practice.

• Find a meditation teacher to help you stay honest in your practice. All of us, no matter how experienced we are, can easily go off the track and get lost in our practice. A good meditation teacher can act as a clear mirror to show you where you are and has the skill to point you in a productive direction in your practice. Even the most experienced mindfulness practitioners I know still work with a teacher every now and then to help deepen their practice.

• Allow yourself opportunities for more intensive practice. You can go to insight and Zen meditation centers for formal meditation retreats for as little as a day or for many months. Intensive practice helps strengthen concentration and lets us understand our minds very deeply.

• Any meditative practice, including mindfulness, can bring up emotional and psychological issues. Please incorporate the creative use of counseling or psychotherapy as an adjunct to your practice, particularly if you are doing intensive formal meditation.

- Balance your formal and informal practice every day. These two practices need each other, and each makes the other stronger.

- In one of the following sections, "The Five Mindfulness Trainings," you will be introduced to one of the strongest tools for informal mindfulness practice. Please allow it to guide you as you continue to practice the art of mindful living.

TRANSFORMING SUFFERING

D o you remember seeing cartoons about this family scenario? The wife (or husband) has had a bad day at work, perhaps her boss has yelled at her. She comes home, gets angry, and yells at her spouse. The spouse, in turn, gets angry at the oldest child and yells at her; she then gets angry at her younger sibling and yells at him; he has no one younger to get angry at, so he explodes at the family dog and hits it. The result is an angry, suffering family; nobody feels good.

This scenario illustrates one of the most basic lessons of life: What we do comes back to us. In this case, anger begets anger. In India and most Asian countries (and increasingly in the West), this is known as the Law of Karma, or cause and effect. The Buddha felt that understanding this was so fundamental that he required all of his monks and nuns to contemplate it every day. Each morning, after contemplating the impermanent nature of their bodies, their life spans, and everything else in the material world, the monks and nuns would contemplate this: "My actions are my only true possessions. I cannot escape the consequences of my actions. My actions are the ground on which I stand."

Our actions have consequences. Most of the time, we are unaware of any except perhaps the most immediate of these consequences. We are like a person who has dropped a pebble into a pond and can only see, at best, one ripple the pebble made in the water. We know from our experience that the pebble actually causes many ripples, perhaps an infinite number, that extend all the way from the spot where it was dropped in the water to the edge of the pond. As the family scenario shows us, our actions have as many consequences as the water has ripples. As the result of the wife's boss's anger, the family dog was hit. Perhaps the dog suffered a physical injury. We know some husbands would not have stopped at yelling at their wives, but might have hit them. The boss's anger would then have had further consequences. The wife would have gone to the hospital, a doctor at the hospital would have had to work an extra shift because of another domestic abuse patient, the children at the doctor's home would not have had dinner with her that night and would have felt the loss of her company, and so on. All these consequences came from one outburst of anger.

Each person in the chain of karma also has a choice about how to act. For example, when most of us look at this scenario, what we see is that the wife has dumped the boss's anger on her husband, who in turn dumped it on his daughter, and so on. But the situation is a little different, as we have learned over the past ten weeks. The husband, daughter, son, and even the dog all have the seeds of anger in them, just as the wife does. When the boss stimulated the wife's seed of anger at work, it got very large and out of control. When she showed her anger, she touched the seed of anger in her husband and his anger exploded. The implications of this understanding are that each person in the chain can choose whether or not to act out the seed of anger within him or her. The husband could have listened to his wife's anger, told her how much it hurt him for her to be angry with him like that, and then asked her what had made her so angry. This would have given her the opportunity to touch the seed of her hurt as well as her seed of healing. Perhaps she could have also seen how wrong it was for her to yell at her husband. (If not, he should have reminded her of this!)

In this revised scenario, the husband has chosen not to carry along the karma of anger but to counteract it with actions of strength, self-confidence, love, and compassion. By doing this, he has created a different karma. One consequence of his actions would be a calmer household. As we can see, there would also be other consequences, perhaps not seen or noticed at the time but just as important.

For the husband to act in this way, he would have to have some understanding of himself, his own patterns of behavior, and his spouse and her patterns of behavior. This would be a bit unusual. Most of the time, most of us are running on autopilot: We react to situations out of our old habit energies, without any real understanding or awareness of what we're doing, why we're doing it, or what the consequences of our actions are.

This is where the practices you've been doing over the past ten weeks can help you. If you have been practicing mindfulness, you are a lot more likely to have developed some awareness of yourself, your world, and the way your mind works. You are more likely to be aware of the pre-conceptions and old reactive patterns you bring to the situation. And once you are aware of those patterns, you can step around them. You can welcome them, embrace them, and not act (or react) out of them. Your practices of mindfulness help you create some space around your thoughts, feelings, and perceptions. You might even experience this as a sense of spaciousness within your mind, or a sense that your skull is larger than your brain and that your brain has some space around it. Whatever the sensation is, the result is that you have some breathing room. Once you have breathing room, you can see the situation in front of you more clearly, and you can act in helpful, constructive ways.

When you hear people say that spiritual practices like mindfulness can help change your karma, this is part of what they are referring to. When we approach life without awareness, we allow our karma to run us — that is, we unconsciously play out the consequences of our actions, our thoughts, our feelings, and our habit energy, which has been building up throughout our lives (or if you accept reincarnation, over our many lives). When the light of mindfulness is strong enough to illuminate our habitual reactions, we can act in more mindful ways, and when we do this, we break the pattern of our old karma — we change it.

For the Buddha, the cause-and-effect nature of actions, or karma, was a subset of the more general, fundamental nature of the phenomenal world: "This is because that is," the Buddha said; "this is not because that is not." Things happen and manifest because the causes and conditions that allow them to happen are present (anger begets anger). When those causes and conditions go away, others arise and something else manifests or happens (compassion begets compassion). Nothing in the cosmos is independent of anything else; everything relies on causes and conditions for its very existence. All things "inter-are." Nothing remains the same forever because the causes and conditions change. All things are impermanent. We have already experienced something of interbeing and impermanence in our practices over the past several weeks, especially the guided meditations on feelings, thinking, and objects of mind in the sixth, seventh, and eighth weeks. It is not much of a leap to apply that experience to our actions.

Once we do this, we can see how deeply our actions and the actions of others affect our futures and the futures of our children. We can see that karma is both an individual and a collective matter. Our actions are the results of causes and conditions from others, and the actions of others are the results of causes and conditions from us. If we can change our actions, we can create a chain of events that will change the karma of many beings.

When the Buddha saw how all things inter-are, he realized what causes suffering and what can transform suffering into joy — in essence, he saw how we can liberate ourselves from our negative karma and uncover our joyful and spacious true nature. To give us the direct experience of that transformation, he taught four basic understandings that he called the "Four Noble Truths."

The First Noble Truth is that suffering exists. We all know this because we all experience it. The word the Buddha used for suffering was *dukkha,* which in the

Buddha's day referred to the condition of a cart with one wheel that didn't work quite right. "Suffering" here means not just hunger, disease, anger, or oppression, although it certainly does mean those things; it also means the anguish we feel when our lives are not going quite right or when something is missing in our understanding of ourselves or our situation.

Once we acknowledge that suffering exists, we may feel relief (I know I did). Now we don't have to fight suffering off anymore or feel as though something is wrong about us that we experience suffering. A capricious god or blind fate has not picked us out to suffer. Suffering is a basic condition of life. We all encounter it. Even the Buddha encountered suffering. He left his comfortable life as a prince because he experienced suffering and wanted to get to the root of it. So we are all in this same boat together, the boat of existence in the phenomenal world, the boat aboard which suffering exists and on which we encounter it. The practices we have been doing, including becoming aware of areas of discomfort in our bodies, developing awareness of the feelings that lie within our discomfort, and becoming more aware of our thought patterns, including judgment and anger, are all different ways of touching the reality of suffering in our lives in a way that we can handle. These practices become our way of developing an awareness of the true nature of our suffering.

If we do our practices correctly, we maintain a balance between suffering and joy. The guided meditations in this book remind us that smiling to our pain is essential if we are not to drown in it. Drowning or wallowing in our suffering is not developing an awareness of suffering. We all spend time in the sewer, but most of us don't know anything else, and most of us don't know of what, exactly, the sewer consists. All we know is, we're suffering.

As we develop an awareness of our suffering, we also begin to understand the true nature of our suffering, which means understanding what caused it. Remember that everything arises because of causes and conditions. Suffering is also the result of this cause-and-effect nature of the phenomenal world. This is the Second Noble Truth. Suffering has causes and conditions just like everything else, and the primary causes and conditions of suffering are attachment, aversion, and the kinds of "nourishments" to which we expose ourselves.

Attachment and aversion we have already begun to explore in the last three sections of this book. Continuing and developing these practices is essential to our deepening awareness of the nature of our minds and our habit energies. Many of the guided meditations in Thich Nhat Hanh's *The Blooming of a Lotus* and many of the suggestions for sitting practice in Jack Kornfield's *A Path with Heart* are helpful guides as we further this practice of deep looking.

I also referred to "nourishments." What does that mean? By "nourishments," I am not just referring to edible food; I am also referring to feelings, conversations, media, willfulness, anything we all encounter on any level. Everything we encounter can become a cause or condition for us to think, feel, or act in certain ways. Do you remember my description of the mind in the sixth week (meditations on feelings)? I described the mind as having a mind consciousness and a storehouse consciousness, and the storehouse consciousness as having "seeds." The nourishments the Buddha referred to in the Second Noble Truth are those things that nourish or stimulate seeds in our storehouse consciousness. Practicing with the Second Noble Truth means developing an increasing awareness of how everything we expose ourselves to affects us. The formal and informal practices of mindfulness are essential to developing this kind of awareness.

The Third Noble Truth follows from the second: There is a way out of suffering. Another way of saying this would be "There is more to life than suffering." Life contains suffering, but it also contains joy, love, kindness, and compassion. The Third Noble Truth helps to point us in a direction: We want to transform suffering, but into what?

Over the last several weeks you have practiced embracing your difficult feelings and thoughts with acceptance and compassion. You have used a smile to express your loving attitude toward your worst garbage. As you have touched these areas of suffering with mindfulness, you may have experienced that your attitude of acceptance toward your pain and discomfort has given rise to compassion and caring. For most of us, the natural process of transformation of suffering is that it turns into and nourishes compassion, loving-kindness, joy, and equanimity. In Buddhist literature, these four qualities are called the "Four Brahmaviharas." Their Sanskrit names are *maitri* (loving-kindness, also *metta*), *karuna* (compassion), *mudita* (joy), and *uppeksha* (equanimity, also *upekkha*).

So perhaps suffering is like a jewel in the rough. We enter deeply into the coal dust, and diamonds reveal themselves to us. I can't stress enough that this process of transformation is spontaneous. Please don't try to make it happen. Just water the seeds of your mindfulness to help keep it strong, embrace your suffering with your mindfulness, and let it do its work.

One idea I've heard often is that transforming suffering means becoming detached and emotionally neutral. In that view, the goal seems to be to observe suffering from a distance, not to feel it directly; then, if we don't feel suffering, we don't feel anything else, either. That is suppression, and it is not a helpful way to practice. You don't want to become disconnected from life. Your practices over the last ten weeks have shown you that you can enter deeply into the experience of the moment, be completely one with it, and not be annihilated. You have discovered that the key to entering deeply into your suffering and difficult feelings is to maintain a balance — not to shy away from suffering, and at the same time, to do practices that nourish joy and happiness within you. You have also observed that whatever it was that you entered into changed during the time you were mindful of it. That change is transformation, which can only happen if you engage yourself fully and directly in the experience of the present moment.

The Buddha suggests to us that if we want to transform our suffering, we first need to look deeply into the causes and conditions that created it. Then, once we have done this, we can assist transformation by exposing ourselves to healthful nourishments. For an abused child to transform his suffering, for example, he might first have to remove himself from the environment where he is exposed to the "nourishments" of physical and emotional abuse. For a person who works for a television news

186 BEGINNING MINDFULNESS

program and finds herself becoming jaded and cynical, transforming her suffering may start with exposing herself to "nourishments" that inspire hope, faith, and joy in herself to counteract the exposure she has in her work to "nourishments" of anger, hatred, fear, and callousness.

Breaking free of the nourishments of suffering is virtually impossible. We would have to live in a completely different world for that to happen. Just waking up and walking out the door exposes us to toxic nourishments: polluted air and noise if we live in the city, the suffering of a fly being eaten by a frog if we live in the country. Developing practices that help us nourish positive seeds in the storehouse consciousness is essential. The practices in Thich Nhat Hanh's *Teachings on Love* and Sharon Salzberg's books on metta or loving-kindness meditation are particularly helpful guides.

Mindfulness is a positive seed in the storehouse consciousness. Strengthening our mindfulness is essential if we are to embrace our suffering and not drown in it. By nourishing mindfulness, we can make it strong enough to embrace the suffering and help it transform. We have explored this process throughout the ten sections of this book. Continuing these practices and developing the practices suggested in any of the books in "Recommended Reading" will strengthen mindfulness.

The Fourth Noble Truth tells us how to lead a life that creates causes and conditions leading to joy rather than suffering. It is known as the Noble Eightfold Path: Right View, Right Understanding, Right Mindfulness, Right Concentration, Right Effort, Right Livelihood, Right Speech, and Right Action. Engaging in the practices of mindfulness with persistence and ever deepening attention will lead us to understand each aspect of the Noble Eightfold Path. More concretely, we can enact the Noble Eightfold Path by practicing the Five Mindfulness Trainings, which we explore in the next section of this book. For a more detailed introduction to the Noble Eightfold Path, Thich Nhat Hanh's *The Heart of the Buddha's Teaching* and Seung Sahn's *Compass of Zen* offer differing and complementary approaches. Each step we take along the path of mindfulness shows us that our practice of mindfulness does not just benefit us. We are at this moment the recipients of the karma of all actions that have come before us, and each action we take contains consequences that will affect all who come after us. Please don't get paralyzed by this; for most people I know who practice mindfulness and have come to this awareness, it is quite liberating. After all, I am not the only person whose thoughts and actions will affect what happens; this is true of everyone. I am not the only person from whom everything originates; things originate from everyone. The living realization of interbeing means that at some level we understand that we are not alone or separate; if I am responsible to you, then you are also responsible to me.

None of us can live a life in which every action creates only positive consequences. At best, the consequences of each action we take will be mixed. All we can do is to live as mindfully as possible and to expand our horizons so that we start seeing more and more of the ripples in the pond when we drop that pebble. As we practice the art of mindful living, a spaciousness will open up for us around our feelings, thoughts, and perceptions, and we will be less likely to be reactive to the situations of our lives. When we are reactive, we carry forward the karma of what is given us in that moment, whether good or bad. When we can live more mindfully, we become better at choosing how to act, and we have the potential to create a better situation for everyone. As we transform our suffering, everybody benefits. As we liberate ourselves from the awful effects of our karma, we liberate everyone.

THE FIVE MINDFULNESS TRAININGS

I n the practice we call "mindfulness," mindfulness itself is the first step. Mindfulness is the energy of awakening. When true mindfulness is present, a deep concentration arises in which we are one with whatever we are aware of, whether it's our breath, the sound of a passing car, our feelings of joy or sadness, and so on. As our concentration deepens, as we penetrate deeply into the heart of the object of our concentration and we have that "Aha!" experience of an opening or understanding that arises clearly within us, we experience insight. In various talks the Buddha referred to these three aspects of mindfulness practice as mindfulness *(sati)*, concentration *(samadhi)*, and insight *(vipassana)*.

Mindfulness is the energy or state of being within which concentration and insight arise. You have already tasted the fruit of mindfulness in your practice every time you maintain your attention on your breathing. As you experienced the change in your breathing and the space that opens within you with each breath, you experienced concentration, a oneness with the object of your attention. As you further deepen your practice of mindfulness, one of the insights that arises is the experience of the disintegration of your sense of isolation. You may notice this in a sense of spaciousness within you that incorporates the sounds or sights around you, even if just for an instant. Or you may be looking at or talking with someone and suddenly know inside you what it is like to be that person.

This is normal. Mindfulness practice incorporates the understanding that we are not separate from each other. This awareness of oneness, of nonduality, is fundamental to true mindfulness practice. This fundamental understanding has far-reaching implications about how we live our lives and interact in the world. It is frequently known by a rather clumsy name, "interdependent co-arising." I find it easier to refer to it as "interbeing."

Interbeing has its origins in one of the Buddha's great contributions to spiritual knowledge. The Buddha saw that nothing within us remains the same throughout time and space. We are like a wave on the water. The wave arises and passes away. The water in the wave doesn't stay together in some fashion and become another wave; it returns to the ocean and gets mixed up with all the rest of the water. So it is with any manifestation we encounter: people, animals, plants, minerals, even thoughts and feelings. Each of these is the water thrusting itself forth in a particular form. Each water molecule is part of each wave. Without the water molecules at the bottom of the ocean, the wave could not exist — it would fall back into the ocean immediately. The Buddha even taught that no "water" remains the same throughout time and space. We can only know "water" through its form: ocean, stream, pond, wave. "Water" has no existence outside of its manifestations.

The basis of our suffering, the Buddha explained, is that we confuse the wave with the water. We are like a wave that tries to keep itself together in one piece when it crashes on the shore. We are attached to our "waveness." We fear that if the wave disperses, we will be annihilated. We forget that the wave is made up of water, and that water is completely interconnected with the rest of the water. As Thich Nhat Hanh likes to remind us, the water, unlike the wave, is never "born" and it never "dies." From this misunderstanding comes loneliness, isolation, fear of death, and our mistreatment of ourselves, others, and the world.

Once we have experienced this understanding, we can no longer view ourselves as separate. We begin to understand that everything we do has an impact. Claude AnShin Thomas, a Zen monk and teacher who is also a Vietnam War combat veteran, speaks of his experience of having been the one who shot the bullet and the one who was shot at, of being the prisoner and the prison guard, of being the hunter and the hunted. When we do eating meditation, we have the opportunity to see how our food contains so many things: the earth, the sun, water, the animal, the farmer, the farmer's family, the ants and spiders. We eat this food and take all of that into ourselves. When we watch television, we can practice "television meditation." If we watch reports of violence on the news, we ingest fighting, killing, and suffering; when we watch a commercial for perfume, we ingest a particular presentation of sexuality; when we listen to music, we ingest the music. Like physical food, some of these are nourishing and some are toxic. We watch and listen and take all of that into ourselves.

At what point can we say we are separate and distinct? Look at your hand. In your hand are your mother and father. You contain their chromosomes and are literally their flesh and blood. Where did your mother and father come from? Their parents. How far back can you extend your lineage? Back to the earliest humans, to the earliest life-forms on this planet, to the origins of the earth, the origins of the solar system. You are made of the stuff of stars, black holes, and interstellar space. You are made of rocks, dirt, and water. Your human ancestors are the same as those of the people you most despise as well as those you most love. Look deeply into yourself and you will find you contain everything. You cannot exist without it, and it cannot exist without you. Inside the wave, you are the water.

This is interbeing. The implications of this under-standing are simple: Every time we mistreat anything, we mistreat ourselves. Every time we take care of someone else, we take care of ourselves. When we take good care of ourselves, we take good care of the universe. When we despoil our environment, we pollute ourselves. To live in true mindfulness means to live naturally and unself-consciously with this reality. When we live like this, our awareness leads us to act harmoniously with the world around us. We can no more ignore suffering outside us than we can ignore suffering inside us. To live in this way, enacting mindfulness in our lives, engages our practice in the world and leads us to deeper understandings of our-selves and everything around us.

What is the role of the Five Mindfulness Trainings in this process? Initially the Buddha oriented his teachings toward monastics — monks and nuns. When one of his first nonmonastic students asked the Buddha how a layperson could practice the path of awakening, the Buddha offered him something he called the "Five Precepts." In his description of the three-stage process leading to awakening (Mindfulness or Precepts → Concentration → Insight), the Buddha used the words for mindfulness *(sati)* and precepts *(sila)* interchangeably, so he was offering those precepts as a way to establish mindfulness in daily life. Thich Nhat Hanh renamed the Five Precepts "The Five Mindfulness Trainings," and I use that name because it is in keeping with the Buddha's teaching that to practice the Five Precepts is to train ourselves in practicing mindfulness.

The Five Mindfulness Trainings present us with guideposts for living a truly mindful life from a core understanding of interbeing. Because everything contains everything else, because everything depends on everything else, we must practice great awareness, love, compassion, and care in our lives. This understanding is the fruit of mindful-ness and concentration. Therefore, to practice the Five Mindfulness Trainings means to practice the kind of true mindfulness that contains stillness, insight, and true awakening.

The Five Mindfulness Trainings are ways to train ourselves in the practice of mindfulness. They can only help us if we enter into an organic, growing relationship with them and use them as practice tools. We can consider the Five Mindfulness Trainings as both daily-life mindfulness guides and as subjects for sitting meditation. For example, we might one day consider the First Mindfulness Training in everything we do:

> Aware of the suffering caused by the destruction of life, I am committed to cultivate compassion and learn ways to protect the lives of people, animals, plants, and minerals. I am determined not to kill, not to let others kill, and not to condone any act of killing in the world, in my thinking and in my way of life.

In what way are we killing? When we boil water, we kill microbes. When we walk, we crush ants. In what ways do we "kill" in our thinking? When we judge ourselves or mentally criticize someone, we are killing with our mind. To practice the First Mindfulness Training is to make the commitment to spend every moment being aware of killing and allowing our understanding of killing to grow and change.

Of course, we know that we most likely will not maintain that awareness every moment. We also suspect that we cannot ever live completely by the Five Mindfulness Trainings. Even if we are vegetarians and pacifists, we still cannot live the First Mindfulness Training completely. We still kill every day. For example, when we drink water, we ingest microorganisms, which die in our stomachs. We only need to do our best. The Mindfulness Trainings give us the opportunity to develop and increase our understanding. If we find ourselves judging ourselves for not "obeying" the Mindfulness Trainings, we have a good opportunity to notice our judgment thoughts and send ourselves some loving-kindness.

The Five Mindfulness Trainings are not commandments. No divine source will punish us if we "violate" them. So we must take the "Thou shalt" and "Thou shalt not" out of our mental and emotional loop when we consider the Mindfulness Trainings. If we cannot live a Mindfulness Training completely, it does not mean we have failed or that we are sinful; it means we are human, partly awake and partly forgetful. The more we practice the Mindfulness Trainings, the greater our mindfulness will become. We practice the Mindfulness Trainings just as we practice any other form of meditation.

The Mindfulness Trainings remind us that mindfulness practice is not about escaping from the world: How can we escape from something that makes us up? Mindfulness practice gives us the opportunity for ever deepening levels of awareness of interbeing and our own true nature.

The Five Mindfulness Trainings come in many versions. Thich Nhat Hanh translated and embellished the one presented here to reflect the reality of our daily lives. Please do not take the Mindfulness Trainings as dogma; that defeats their purpose. If you wish, allow them to blossom in your life. They are most helpful when they become living entities. Then they can change and transform as we encounter new experiences in our lives, and our living awareness of the Mindfulness Trainings can transform the experiences in our lives.

THE FIVE MINDFULNESS TRAININGS

THE FIRST MINDFULNESS TRAINING. Aware of the suffering caused by the destruction of life, I am committed to cultivate compassion and learn ways to protect the lives of people, animals, plants, and minerals. I am determined not to kill, not to let others kill, and not to condone any act of killing in the world, in my thinking and in my way of life.

THE SECOND MINDFULNESS TRAINING. Aware of the suffering caused by exploitation, social injustice, stealing, and oppression, I am committed to cultivate loving-kindness and learn ways to work for the well-being of people, animals, plants, and minerals. I am committed to practice generosity by sharing my time, energy, and material resources with those who are in real need. I am determined not to steal and not to possess anything that should belong to others. I will respect the property of others, but I will prevent others from profiting from human suffering or the suffering of other species on earth.

THE THIRD MINDFULNESS TRAINING. Aware of the suffering caused by sexual misconduct, I am committed to cultivate responsibility and learn ways to protect the safety and integrity of individuals, couples, families, and society. I am determined not to engage in sexual relations without love and a long-term commitment. To preserve the happiness of myself and others, I am determined to respect my commitments and the commitments of others. I will do everything in my power to protect children from sexual abuse and to prevent couples and families from being broken by sexual misconduct.

THE FOURTH MINDFULNESS TRAINING. Aware of the suffering caused by unmindful speech and the inability to listen to others, I am committed to cultivate loving speech and deep listening in order to bring joy and happiness to others and relieve others of their suffering. Knowing that words can create happiness or suffering, I am committed to learn to speak truthfully, with words that inspire self-confidence, joy, and hope. I am determined not to spread news that I do not know to be certain and not to criticize or condemn things of which I am not sure. I will refrain from uttering words that can cause division or discord, or that can cause the family or community to break. I will make all efforts to reconcile and resolve all conflicts, however small.

THE FIFTH MINDFULNESS TRAINING. Aware of the suffering caused by unmindful consumption, I am committed to cultivate good health, both physical and mental, for myself, my family, and my society by practicing mindful eating, drinking, and consuming. I am committed to ingest only items that preserve peace, well-being, and joy in my body, in my consciousness, and in the collective body and consciousness of my family and society. I am determined not to use alcohol or any other intoxicant or to ingest foods or other items that contain toxins, including certain TV programs, magazines, books, films, and conversations. I am aware that to damage my body or my consciousness with these poisons is to betray my ancestors, my parents, my society, and future generations. I will work to transform violence, fear, anger, and confusion in myself and in society by practicing a diet for myself and for society. I understand that a proper diet is crucial for self-transformation and for the transformation of society.

THE IMPORTANCE OF COMMUNITY

Most people in my mindfulness meditation classes tell me that they find it easier or more fruitful to practice sitting and walking meditation in class than to do it by themselves. They are touching on something important and powerful: the support that others can give us and we can give them in our meditation practice. People who practice all forms of meditation (including mindfulness practice) find the support of a community to be very important.

The fact is, we human beings are mostly more like dogs or elephants than we are like pandas or grizzly bears. Dogs and elephants cannot survive outside of their community; they rely on one another for food, safety, and well-being. Pandas and grizzly bears are mostly solitary, staking out their own territory and spending most of their time alone. Even though aloneness is important for each of us and the silence of being by ourselves is essential for our stability, we humans are communal beings. We may go off on our own for periods of time, but then we come back to be with other humans like us.

The Buddha considered the support of a community of practice to be so important that he saw it as one of three things that are safe havens for living a mindful life. These three are the enlightened or awakened mind that exists in all of us *(buddha);* the reality of things as they are and the teachings that help us uncover the awakened mind so we can see that and free ourselves from suffering *(dharma);* and the community of people who practice the teachings and give each other spiritual support *(sangha).*

Communities of mindfulness practice, or sanghas, function as support for us in maintaining and developing mindfulness in our lives. We get nourishment, support, and guidance from others who have the same intention to wake up, and we have the opportunity to support others as well. Practicing with a group is essential to breaking down the barrier between ourselves and others, helping to ease the delusion that we are separate and alone. It is not too extreme to say that our practice of mindfulness will not survive well if we do not have a community with which to practice. On a day when you're a complete mess, isn't it great to know that you can go to your community and find someone else there who is feeling a bit stronger and who can help you strengthen yourself and your practice? And isn't it great to know that you can return the favor when you are feeling strong and solid in your practice?

As we apply ourselves to developing the habits of mindfulness in daily life, our sangha can give us necessary support. At first, the habits of mindfulness may be like a small toothpick in the path of the freight train of our not-so-mindful habits. As we practice mindfulness more, the toothpick grows and can turn into a large tree. The tree has a chance of stopping the freight train. When our mindfulness is a toothpick, we need the support of others to strengthen our practice, and having a group of people to practice with on a regular basis will help us establish good and helpful habits. When our mindfulness is a strong tree, we can offer that strength and stability to others.

For me, the sangha is a lifeline. I am fortunate enough to have a local sangha where I live and a sangha of people around the country and the world that I get to see less frequently but rely on just as strongly. I rely on my weekly local sangha gatherings for nurturing, support, and guidance, and I rely on my sangha friends around the world for their love and compassion, their phone calls, letters, and emails, and the occasional times when we are all in one place together.

Communities of practice are great supports and great teachers. Each person's experience is valuable and speaks to a truth within us. In conversations in our meditation group, we frequently feel that each one of us is speaking for all of us. And all of our worst and best social habits come up in our practice communities, which gives us a good opportunity to work on our mindful speaking, listening, and acting. When I'm at my worst, behaving like a willful five-year-old or an insecure teenage kid, or being insensitive to others, my sangha reminds me of this in a way I can take in. I have the chance not only to see my behavior and its consequences but also to change them. A good community creates a zone of safety, where we can be ourselves and be with others who are also committed to living an awakened life. My sangha supports me to be my best and accepts me at my worst. What a relief!

So finding a community to practice with is very help-ful. If you live in a community with a spiritual bookstore, you might find a sangha through them. Other good resources are adult education courses (where this book originated). If you can't find a sangha that way, here are a couple of national resources.

Tricycle: The Buddhist Review is a quarterly magazine. It has classified ads and listings of different meditation groups around the country. If you are interested in mind-fulness meditation, look for "insight" or "vipassana" groups or for "Soto Zen" groups.

Shambhala Sun is a bimonthly magazine of Buddhist resources. They also have a website, www.shambhalasun.com, that lists communities of practice in various traditions throughout the United States and Canada.

On the World Wide Web, Thich Nhat Hanh's Unified Buddhist Church has a website listing communities of prac-tice in his tradition around the world: www.iamhome.org. The worldwide Zen communities of Zen Master Seung Sahn are listed on www.kwanumzen.org. Claude AnShin Thomas's communities of practice are listed on www.zaltho.org. My own meditation community has its own website, mem-bers.aol.com/ctsangha, with links to various other related sites. Also, a clearing-site for Buddhist organizations called www.buddhanet.org has links to many communities of many different traditions.

If there really is no community where you are, then you can start your own. The need and interest in your area may surprise you. When I moved from Belmont, Massachusetts, where I had lived for fourteen years, to Maynard, where I knew only a couple of people, I told the

two people I knew that I would be doing sitting meditation at my home one evening and invited anyone to join
me. Eight people showed up the first night. Our sangha
has grown from there.

You do not have to be a meditation teacher to help
create and nurture a sangha. If you have the intention and
desire, you will find that your community will be there. All
you have to do is try. Organizations like the Community
of Mindful Living in California and DharmaFriends in
Hawaii are glad to help by providing encouragement
and materials; sometimes meditation teachers are will-
ing to travel (even to out-of-the-way locations) to provide
support and instruction. And this book can be a good way
to begin a new sangha, because the instructions and practices contained within it can both introduce new people to
the practice and reinvigorate those who are more experienced. I encourage you to do it!

TRUE VOICE

In 1999 I received ordination in the White Plum Buddhist lineage. As part of the ordination, the priest who ordained me, Claude AnShin Thomas, gave me a spiritual name. The name he chose for me was JiYu, which means to have faith or confidence in one's own self as a manifestation of the true nature of the universe. Like most well-chosen spiritual names, it is both a reflection of who I am and a challenge for my spiritual growth. What does it mean to have faith in my own self in that way?

I have come to understand that the name JiYu represents one of the keys to good mindfulness practice: the understanding that we are simply becoming more and more completely ourselves, each of us in our own unique way. This is a little different than how most of us begin spiritual practice. In each community I've spent time in, I've noticed that the students tend to imitate the teacher. If the teacher hits the floor with his hand, everyone else hits the floor with his or her hand. If the teacher laughs a certain way or walks at a certain speed or holds her hands out in a particular way, the students will unconsciously do the same thing. This is how we learn initially — monkey-see, monkey-do. I put myself in that same category. When I first met Thich Nhat Hanh, I began walking like him, talking with the same rhythm — all unconsciously. When I first began studying with Zen Master Bo Mun, I would present comments in discussion that sounded a lot like him and found my voice and speech pattern tended to imitate his. We do these things, not because we are clones, but because we see that the teacher has a state of understanding that we want to have, and we figure that if we imitate the teacher, we'll get it. It is like the story told earlier about Mu Deung's attempt to attain true understanding by reading that one sentence in the Diamond Sutra. He imitated someone else. It took his Zen master's challenge, the question "Who are you?" to help him realize that he was approaching this incorrectly.

Imitation may be a way to start, but it is never the correct path. We may go through that phase, but if we really want to grow we need to move out of it. We need to allow our own authentic voice to come forward.

As we continue to unwrap ourselves to the present moment, we reveal what has always been there and become more and more ourselves. My own self may be made of the same elements as yours; we may share the same storehouse consciousness, the same ancestry, the same substance of our true nature; but our manifestations of it are different. In all of our quirky differences lies the truth of the world. All of us are necessary, no one more or less important than any other, and just as we are. If each of our voices is clear and true, then together we make harmony. It may not look or sound like your or my idea of harmony, so let's throw the ideas out the window and just see what is.

My deepest hope is that this little book will nourish you in the complete expression of your own true nature. If you appreciate what I have offered, please allow your own true voice to speak, become aware of the deep truth of who you really are, and manifest that great gift in this world as fully as you can.

We will see each other on the path of practice.

AFTERWORD

I published this book privately from 1996 to 2003. I got feedback from many people who used the book during that period, some of them students of mine and others who used the book on their own. I revised and expanded it several times.

The biggest revisions came in 2000 and 2001. I recalled Zen Master Su Bong's exhortation to me: "Speak from your experience. That's what people want to hear," and I went through the book to make sure that everything I wrote was an expression of my own practice and not simply a recitation of something I had read or heard. As I continue my development on the mindfulness path, and as my practice continues to widen and diversify, I can better express my practice and have confidence in its worth. While I am grounded deeply in Zen practice, I have also studied in other areas as well, some Buddhist and others not. Because I am a natural synthesizer, this book reveals these other influences.

My goal is to honor Su Bong's instruction to me and to present the practices of mindfulness as they work in my life.

The book is primarily Buddhist, probably 99 percent, but not everything in it is an accurate presentation of traditional Buddhist teachings. When you read other Buddhist authors, you may find differences. Here are the most obvious ones.

The sixth week's meditation on feelings includes working with emotions as well as sensations. In the Buddhist tradition, "feelings" refers to the sensations that we experience through our senses. In this book I incorporated the realization that physical sensations in the body are material embodiments of emotional states. This is the result of my studies, not in traditional Buddhist teachings, but in alternative healing and metaphysics, which began with my training under the late Eleanore Moore of Peterborough, New Hampshire, and continues to this day with my training in Sharon Turner's Awakenings program.

Similarly, in the section "Making Choices" and in the fifth and sixth weeks, I separate how to work with emotions and feelings on one hand and the narrative story and thought forms on the other. This reflects the value that I place on the information contained in our emotions, particularly the chronic, repetitive ones. Classic Buddhist teachings do not make this distinction, instead treating emotions no differently than other thought forms or mental formations.

The section "Being Grounded" has no specific reference in Buddhism. I included it because the practice of grounding myself in my body is essential to me, and I suspect, to anyone who wants to live free of chaos. Claude AnShin Thomas emphasizes being grounded in his teachings as well, although our styles of presentation are different, with mine showing the influence of my work with Sharon Turner.

My presentation of metta and tonglin practices reflects how I have adapted these practices to my own use. My approach does not reflect how one would teach those practices in their classical traditions.

One dilemma that many of us face as Buddhism and mindfulness make their transition to Western culture is how to bring together Buddhist teachings with our own Western (and frequently psychologically based) under-standings of human behavior and how to continue to own our background in the Judeo-Christian tradition. The Buddha's understanding of human beings is timeless and true. The understandings of Western psychology and eso-teric traditions, including Native American ones, are equally valid and have different emphases. This book reflects one way of working out this synthesis.

This book remains a basic introduction to practice. Other teachers have explored in greater depth the mind-fulness practices presented here. I am honored that your exploration of mindfulness has begun here; I surely hope it does not end here!

In gratitude I offer this book at the feet of the great teachers whom I have the joy to learn from in my life. May all beings be safe, joyful, and strong, and may the merit of this book be for the benefit of all.

PERMISSIONS ACKNOWLEDGMENTS

I am deeply grateful to those whose quotes appear in this book or whose work I have adapted here for their insight and skill in presenting the teachings of mindfulness:

To Harrison Hoblitzelle for the first version of the list of daily-life mindfulness activities that appears in the "First Week" section.

To Robert Aitken, Roshi, for the gathas "Problems at Work" and "Going to Sleep" from his book *The Dragon Who Never Sleeps* (Parallax Press, copyright © Robert Aitken, 1992).

To Richard Borofsky and Antra Kalnins Borofsky for their wonderful quotation on faith that appears in the "First Week" section. Richard and Antra run the Center for the Study of Relationship at 86 Washington Avenue, Cambridge, Massachusetts 02140, telephone 617-661-7890. The quotation is from their Fall 1997–Spring 1998 brochure.

To the Venerable Thich Nhat Hanh, for the following quotations in this book: the gatha "Listen, Listen" from *Present Moment, Wonderful Moment* (Parallax Press, copyright © Thich Nhat Hanh, 1990); the gatha "I have arrived, I am home" from *The Mindfulness Bell,* volume 10 (Winter 1994, copyright © Community of Mindful Living, 1994); the gatha "Hugging" from *Present Moment, Wonderful Moment* (Parallax Press, copyright © Thich Nhat Hanh, 1990); the gatha meditation on calming body and mind from *The Blooming of a Lotus* (Beacon Press, copyright © Thich Nhat Hanh, 1993); and the text of the Five Mindfulness Trainings (not the commentary on the text, which is my own) from *For a Future to Be Possible* (Parallax Press, copyright © Thich Nhat Hanh, 1993). The guided meditation on the body that Thich Nhat Hanh and the monks, nuns, and lay dharma teachers who teach in his tradition have developed is the basis for the one in this book.

To Jack Kornfield, for his pioneering work in adapting the practices of mindfulness to the West. I was delighted to find that he is using a similar process to my first guided meditation on objects of mind in his contemplative psychotherapy practice. He spoke of this in an interview in *Tricycle* magazine (volume IX, no. 4, Summer 2000). I liked his wording for the four questions and have adopted it. (My original wording was "Does this create suffering or well-being? What is this made of? Where does this come from? Who am I?")

To Pema Chödrön for her compassionate and dedicated teaching and for delineating so clearly the four steps of tonglin practice in her book *When Things Fall Apart* (Shambhala Press, copyright © Pema Chödrön, 1997).

RECOMMENDED READING

In my classes I encourage all of us not to read too much. When we find ourselves in doubt, going back to the practices with wholehearted sincerity is usually the best teacher. However, my students have the class to come to, and they have another person who is a little further along the path to encourage them.

I find some books to be helpful adjuncts. If you must read something in conjunction with this book, I strongly suggest these. They can help you a great deal if you use them as practice guides.

Aitken, Robert. *The Dragon Who Never Sleeps: Verses for Zen Buddhist Practice.* Berkeley, Calif.: Parallax Press, 1992. A book of gathas by one of the foremost living Zen teachers in the West.

Braza, Jerry. *Moment by Moment: The Art and Practice of Mindfulness.* Boston, Mass.: Charles E. Tuttle Co., 1997. A useful guide to mindfulness in daily life from a noted university professor and business consultant.

Hanh, Thich Nhat. *The Long Road Turns to Joy: A Guide to Walking Meditation.* Berkeley, Calif.: Parallax Press, 1996. A compact but big book on the art and practice of walking meditation by the master who brought this practice to the West.

―――. *The Miracle of Mindfulness: A Manual on Meditation.* Boston, Mass.: Beacon Press, 1996. An excellent primer on mindfulness practice in everyday life.

―――, et al. *Present Moment, Wonderful Moment: Mindfulness Verses for Daily Living.* Berkeley, Calif.: Parallax Press, 1990. A book of gathas used to help focus attention during formal meditation and daily life.

Kabat-Zinn, Jon. *Wherever You Go, There You Are: Mindfulness Meditation in Everyday Life.* New York: Hyperion Books, 1994. A basic primer on mindfulness practice from the director of the Institute of Mind-fulness in Worcester, Massachusetts.

As you go on, you may find some other books helpful and encouraging. Here are a very few:

Beck, Charlotte Joko. *Everyday Zen: Love and Work.* San Francisco: Harper San Francisco, 1989. A collection of encouraging and insightful talks centered around practice and everyday life.

Chödrön, Pema. *The Wisdom of No Escape: And the Path of Loving-Kindness.* Boston, Mass.: Shambhala Press, 1991, and *When Things Fall Apart: Heart Advice for Difficult Times.* Boston, Mass.: Shambhala Press, 1997.

Both books are wonderful companions for the times when life and practice gets tough. Each has a great chapter on tonglin practice.

Glassman, Bernard. *Instructions to the Cook: A Zen Master's Lessons in Living a Life That Matters,* New York: Bell Tower Books, 1996, and *Bearing Witness: A Zen Master's Lessons in Making Peace.* New York: Bell Tower Books, 1998. Glassman is a pioneer in engaging the practices of mindfulness in daily life. *Bearing Witness* especially provides concrete examples of how mindfulness can make a difference both in interpersonal relationships and in a wider social context.

Hanh, Thich Nhat. *Being Peace,* Berkeley, Calif.: Parallax Press, 1996, and *Touching Peace: Practicing the Art of Mindful Living,* Berkeley, Calif.: Parallax Press, 1992. How to bring peacefulness and joy into daily life and how to handle our suffering, with a focus on individual, family, and community practice.

————. *The Blooming of a Lotus: Guided Meditation Exercises for Healing and Transformation.* Boston, Mass.: Beacon Press, 1993. A book of gatha-guided meditations that go into the more transformative and psychological aspects of mindfulness practice. This is a worthwhile reference as well as a course of study.

————. *Transformation and Healing: The Sutra on the Four Establishments of Mindfulness.* Berkeley, Calif.: Parallax Press, 1990. The full text of the Buddha's sutra "The Four Establishments of Mindfulness" with useful commentary and exercises.

————, ed. *For a Future to Be Possible: Commentaries on the Five Mindfulness Trainings.* Berkeley, Calif.: Parallax Press, 1998. A compendium of essays and commentaries on the Five Mindfulness Trainings by Thich Nhat Hanh, Jack Kornfield, Richard Baker, Joan Halifax, Maxine Hong Kingston, and many others.

Kornfield, Jack. *A Path with Heart: A Guide through the Perils and Promises of Spiritual Life.* New York: Doubleday Books, 1993. A series of meditation teachings in the insight (vipassana) tradition from one of its most prominent teachers in the United States.

Rosenberg, Larry, and David Guy. *Breath by Breath: The Liberating Practice of Insight Meditation.* Boston, Mass.: Shambhala Press, 1998. This is a very helpful book on establishing the practice of mindfulness of breathing by a skillful insight meditation teacher. It is based on the Buddha's text "Sutra on the Full Awareness of Breathing."

Sharon Salzberg. *Loving-Kindness: The Revolutionary Art of Happiness,* Boston, Mass.: Shambhala Press, 1995, and *A Heart As Wide As The World: Living with Mindfulness, Wisdom, and Compassion,* Boston, Mass.: Shambhala Press, 1997. Two lovely books by the foremost teacher of loving-kindness (metta) meditation in the United States.

Seung Sahn. *The Compass of Zen.* Boston, Mass.: Shambhala Press, 1997, and Seung Sahn and Thich Nhat Hanh. *The Heart of the Buddha's Teaching.* Berkeley, Calif.: Parallax Press, 1998. These two volumes offer a comprehensive overview of Buddhist teachings in very different and complementary ways.

Suzuki, Shunryu. *Zen Mind, Beginner's Mind.* Boston, Mass.: Charles E. Tuttle Co., 1997. A big little book of teachings on the Zen art of mindfulness *(shikantaza)* by one of the foremost teachers of this type of Zen in the United States.

Index

U

Unified Buddhist Church, 202
uppeksha (equanimity), 184

V

Vietnam, walking meditation in, 28
vipassana (insight), 189

W

waking up, 13–14
gathas for, 45–46
walking meditation, 26–31
body awareness during, 29–30, 42
in daily life, 15
"don't know" practice during, 55
gathas for, 30–31, 46
groundedness during, 70
home play for, 35, 74, 120–21, 169
for nourishing mindfulness, 80–81

slow walking *(kinhin),* 27–28, 29, 120
washing dishes
and eating meditation, 66
gathas for, 46
Washington (D.C.) Mindfulness Community, 16
Western culture, Buddhism adapted to, 211
Wherever You Go, There You Are (Kabat-Zinn), xxii
who am I?/what is this? *See* "don't know" mind
witness consciousness, 112–13
workplace
daily-life mindfulness at, 15, 16
gathas for, 48

Z

Zen Buddhism, xix, 31
and awareness of thinking, 116–17
meditation centers, 175, 202
mindfulness in, 134

ABOUT THE AUTHOR

Andrew JiYu Weiss has studied mindfulness meditation for many years in the United States, Europe, and Asia. His early studies of Zen focused on the Korean tradition with Zen Master Seung Sahn and Zen Master Su Bong. In 1989 he met the Vietnamese Zen monk Thich Nhat Hanh, and in 1991, he was ordained a Brother in Thich Nhat Hanh's Order of Interbeing. He is a founder of the Community of Interbeing in Boston/Cambridge, Massachusetts, and is the founder and practice coordinator of the Clock Tower Sangha in Maynard, Massachusetts. In 1999 he took ordination in the White Plum Lineage of the Japanese Soto Zen tradition.

Andrew regularly teaches mindfulness meditation at Cambridge Center for Adult Education and at yoga centers in eastern Massachusetts. He is the former instructor of mindfulness practice and client management at the

New England School of Whole Health Education, where he also served as dean of students. His eclectic background includes education and training in optics, law, and conflict resolution, and he continues to work as a dispensing optician, mediator, and consultant to other lawyers.

Andrew offers an individually supervised course of Beginning Mindfulness to a small number of people. This intensive course includes weekly telephone interviews with Andrew. For more information, see www.beginning mindfulness.com or contact Andrew through New World Library.

Andrew lives in Maynard, Massachusetts, with his wife, Avril Rama Bell, herself a longtime student of Siddha Yoga meditation and a gifted intuitive counselor and teacher, and their Tibetan terrier, Shakti.

New World Library is dedicated to
publishing books and audio products
that inspire and challenge us to improve
the quality of our lives and our world.

Our products are available
in bookstores everywhere.
For our catalog, please contact:

New World Library
14 Pamaron Way
Novato, California 94949

Phone: (415) 884-2100 or (800) 972-6657
Catalog requests: Ext. 50
Orders: Ext. 52
Fax: (415) 884-2199

Email: escort@newworldlibrary.com
Website: www.newworldlibrary.com